Iceberg De

Gregory

SPECIAL NOTICE TO ALL READERS

Thank you for your prayerful preview of the pilot version of **Iceberg Dead Ahead**. In all my years of writing, I've never sensed more urgency than in the writing of these pages. I do ask readers to bear in mind that this copy is an incomplete pilot version that is not yet fully edited. The final version will contain about 100 additional pages of the positive solutions and practical steps for turning today's evil tide. However, this early pilot version has been effective for creating urgency and new directions for many. I would deeply appreciate any input from those who read this tool.

Toward the next great awakening,
Dr. Gregory Frizzell

Additional Resources Available from Dr. Frizzell

Returning to Holiness: *A Personal and Church-wide Journey to Revival*

How to Develop A Powerful Prayer Life: *The Biblical Path to Holiness and Relationship with God*

Local Associations and United Prayer: *"Keys To The Coming Revival"*

Biblical Patterns for Powerful Church Prayer Meetings: *"God's Changeless Path to Sweeping Revival and Evangelism"*

Prayer Evangelism for the Local Church: *"One Church's Miraculous Story of Blessing and Deliverance"*

America — Revival, Judgment or Both? *Recognizing and Reversing the Twenty-five Devastating Signs of the Times*

Healthy Relationships, Healed Families and United Churches: *"A Personal and Church-wide Journey to the Heart of Revival"*

Escaping the Trap of Lifeless Religion: *"The Joy and Peace of Really Knowing God"*

Seeking the Reviver, Not Just Revival: *"Personal and Corporate Prayers That Bring Sweeping Revival"*

Restoring the "Missing Elements" for Revival, Awakening and Kingdom Growth

Building an Evangelistic, Kingdom-Focused Church Prayer Ministry: *"God's Path to Revival, Discipleship and Evangelism"*

Holiness and Power in Christian Leaders: *"A Leader's Life Journey of Cleansing, Revival and Intimacy with God"*

Loving God Means Loving Each Other: *"Recapturing the Power of Koinonia Fellowship"*

Powerful Marriage and Family Prayer: *"Restoring the Missing Key to Healthy Families and Revived Churches"*

Covenant of Love and Accountability: *"Returning to Biblical Grace and Lordship"*

Saved, Certain and Transformed: *"Journey to Biblical Salvation, Full Assurance and Personal Revival"*

Dynamic Church Prayer Meetings: *"Why Every Church Must Embrace Them!"*

Empower Us O God: *"A Leader's Manual for Acts 1:8 Evangelism, Ministry and Prayer"*

Perfect Peace: *"How to Never Again Doubt Your Salvation"*

Abiding In Christ: *"Dynamic Daily Prayer and Intimacy with Christ"*

In Remembrance of Me: *"Embracing Lord's Suppers that Change Churches"*

Miraculous Church Unity and Kingdom Vision: *"Journey to Biblical Fellowship and Sweeping Revival"*

Revival Living By Grace Through Faith: *"The Believer's Identify and Union in Christ"*

Sunday, School, Small Groups and Kingdom Prayer: *"The Dawning of a Revival Revolution"*

Seeking God To Seek A Pastor: *"Vital Steps for Search Committees and Their Congregations"*

To Schedule Church or Region-wide Conference

For information concerning conferences or resources contact Dr. Frizzell at:
Baptist General Convention of Oklahoma
3800 N. May Ave., Oklahoma City, OK 73112-6506
phone: 405.942.3800 e-mail: gfrizzell@bgco.org

Conference Titles

- ➢ "Turning Pastor Search into Church-wide Renewal
- ➢ "Going Deeper With God Weekend"
- ➢ Developing Mountain-Moving Prayer and Intimacy with God
- ➢ Journey to Holiness and Power
- ➢ Church and Association-wide Revivals and Solemn Assemblies
- ➢ Transformed Relationships, Healed Families and United Churches
- ➢ Holiness and Power in Christian Leaders
- ➢ Developing Powerful Prayer Meetings and Prayer Ministries
- ➢ Powerful Prayer Meetings and Evangelistic Prayer Ministries
- ➢ Building Dynamic Marriage and Family Prayer
- ➢ Biblical and Historic Patterns of Spiritual Awakening
- ➢ Saved, Certain and Transformed

Iceberg Dead Ahead!

An Urgent Call to "God-Seeking Repentance"

Gregory Frizzell

Iceberg Dead Ahead! "An Urgent Call to "God-Seeking Repentance"
ISBN 978-1-930285-41-5
Copyright © 2007 by Gregory R. Frizzell
Published by The Master Design
    PO Box 569
    Union City, TN 38281-0569
    Bookinfo@masterdesign.org
    www.masterdesign.org

Additional copies of this and other books by Dr. Frizzell may be ordered from:
Baptist General Convention of Oklahoma
3800 N. May Ave., Oklahoma City, OK 73112-6505
phone: 405.942.3800 e-mail: gfrizzell@bgco.org
or online at www.masterdesign.org

All Scripture Quotations, unless otherwise indicated, are taken from the New King James Version. Copyright © 1982 by Thomas Nelson, Inc. Used by permission. All rights reserved. Scriptures quotations marked KJV are from the King James Version of the Bible, part of the public domain.
Printed by Bethany Press International in the USA

The Story of the Cover Artwork

Though the cover photo is not the actual iceberg that sank the RMS Titanic, it bears similarity to descriptions of eye witnesses. Such a sight directly in the path of a liner would strike terror in the heart of any passenger. There is strong evidence the American nation and Church are indeed a spiritual Titanic with a devastating "iceberg dead ahead!" The spiritual iceberg is the deadly consequences of blatant, persistent sin and the imminent judgment of holy God. Yet there is a difference between believers and the Titanic. Through the grace, mercy and power of God, we may yet avoid complete disaster. And even if devastation soon befalls us, there is hope of an ultimate restoration through our covenant in Christ. **Iceberg Dead Ahead** is designed to awaken readers to deep brokenness and repentance while outlining the clear biblical steps of returning to God. Dear saints, the warning is sounded and God's word is clear — repent or perish! (Luke 13:3) The cover picture is used with licensed permission from "PASSPORT STOCK/UNLISTED IMAGES. INC."

Table of **Contents**

Introduction

"America, Titanic and Ignored Warnings"
(Proverbs 29:1)

On the Sunday evening of April 14, 1912 the North Atlantic Ocean was dead calm and cold. The magnificent *Titanic* was making record breaking time on its maiden voyage from Southampton, England to New York City. The ship was unequalled in beauty and so advanced, no thought was given to carrying enough life boats. It was decided more lifeboats would detract from its "aesthetic lines." After all, according to The Shipbuilder Magazine, *Titanic* was thought to be "practically unsinkable." Someone remarked, "even God couldn't sink this ship."

In a lifetime of ship voyages, Captain Edward J. Smith remarked, he had never seen the sea so absolutely calm. The mighty Atlantic Ocean was so still it was described as being "like a millpond." As the sky turned from dusk to deep darkness, some of the most influential people on earth enjoyed the very best of delicacies, music and service. The sunset had been stunning and the stars shone with unusual brilliance. Everything was perfect except for one nagging little inconvenience. The Marconi wireless kept signaling an annoying message — "icebergs in the shipping lane."

Yet this was the Titanic and there were speed records to break. They couldn't let a few icebergs slow this mighty vessel. But the warnings kept coming. They actually started receiving warnings as early as April 12th. Several more ice alerts came throughout the day on the 13th. On the fateful day of April 14th, the first ice warning came at 9:00 am. There was another at 11:40 am, then 1:42 pm and 1:45 pm. They received even more direct warnings at 7:30 pm and again at 9:30 pm.

At 11 pm, the Leyland liner, *Californian* sent an urgent warning of ice in the shipping lane. Because the *California* was only ten miles away, the signal came in so loud, it pierced the ears of wireless operator, George Phillips. The operator was already overwhelmed with piles of unsent casual "wish you were here" type messages from passengers. When he received the ear-splitting warning from the *California*, he angrily tapped the reply, "Shut up, shut up, I am busy!" [1] Incredibly, the engines were kept at full throttle. Then at 11:39 pm a panicked lookout suddenly screamed the cry that forever changed history, "Iceberg Right Ahead!"

And now the unthinkable was in fatal motion. The totally calm sea meant no waves broke at the base of the iceberg. The unusually calm conditions had made it much harder to see the danger. Now it was so close and right in their path! The ship's speed and massive 46,328 tons were now her deadly enemy. Despite their frantic efforts, the huge liner kept plowing forward. The iceberg loomed closer and closer. At the very last instant, the great ship seemed to be turning — they just might make it! Yet at exactly 11:40 pm, a mere thirty seven seconds after the cry rang out, the mighty *Titanic* grazed the ice.

As the iceberg slowly ground past, small chucks fell on the upper decks to be playfully tossed by passengers. It looked like they had made it! After all, they only felt the slightest "little shudder" as they brushed by the berg.[2] Many passengers warm in their beds, were unaware anything had even occurred. But something had indeed occurred! Just two hours and forty minutes later, the *RMS Titanic* slipped beneath the icy sea and fifteen hundred people were tossed into the freezing waters. As 705 people watched in horror from the distant lifeboats, hundreds screamed for help in the deadly cold waters. Within minutes the roar of their cries grew faint and then utterly silent as 1,517 souls slipped into eternity.[3]

But How Could It Have Happened?

For the horrific *Titanic* disaster to have occurred, so many factors had to line up tragically wrong. If any one factor had been even slightly different, the great ship might never have sunk. Perhaps the most fatal factor was the failure to take seriously the ice warnings. Had they taken time to carefully plot each warning by location, they would have realized they were sailing full speed into a virtual "ice field".

But again, they were the "unsinkable" *Titanic* with important people sending and receiving countless wireless messages. They couldn't take the time to seriously plot all those different ice warnings. And besides, who could imagine such a vessel with all its beautiful art and technology actually sinking?[4] Yet had they looked at all the "warnings together," they would have realized the grave danger directly in their path.[5] Is there an analogy between the *Titanic* and the well programmed and high tech American Church? With all our bells and whistles, could America actually sink into the same spiritual abyss as modern Europe? Could our current path force God to act in cataclysmic judgment? Is there an urgent lesson and message we need to hear? Absolutely!

Titanic's Message to America's Church
A Direct and Sobering Analogy

In every life, church and nation, there are fateful moments that change all time and eternity. For the *RMS Titanic* it was when they ignored the last ice warning and kept the engines at full throttle. For the American Church and nation, that time is now! From every direction, the Church has for years received repeated spiritual warnings with little real change in direction. Certainly, we all realize spiritual conditions have been bad and declining for many years. But something has changed! Conditions and signs are suddenly *very different* as many evil factors are now rapidly converging. Like the *Titanic*, we are "surrounded" as never before. A extremely wide range of signs reveal a massive spiritual and social iceberg directly in our path! In many ways, we *are* the Titanic. A central purpose of this book is to try and "put all the warning signs together" to reveal our true position and one hope for change.

Though normally reserved in my pronouncements, I have an overwhelming leading to loudly sound this most urgent alarm and call to repentance. (Isaiah 58:1-2) The opportunity to avoid serious circumstances and judgment may soon be past. Believers, it is unspeakably urgent that we immediately return to God with all our hearts. It is also incumbent that we return to God Himself with pure motives, not merely a selfish desire to "get blessed" or "avoid pain." **Iceberg Dead Ahead** is both a loud alarm and clear outline of the biblical paths of God-seeking repentance. Throughout this book, I use the term "God-seeking" because we must embrace a repentance that is about God's glory and kingdom, *not* merely our own comforts and personal interests. (Ezekiel 33:31; James 4:1-4) In this tool, we will examine the powerful "missing foundations" for returning to God in true repentance and revival. The principles are designed to help saints walk victoriously in blessing or darkness.

Yet while the current moment is incredibly urgent, there may still be a chance for sweeping change. Even if far more serious trials have exploded by the time some read these pages, we can still seek God's face for repentance and revival. While we cannot undo all the consequences, we can turn to the Lord for forgiveness, cleansing and new beginning. In fact, God may well use coming trials to bring us to far deeper readiness for major change. Even under severe judgment, God does not wholly disown those born-again by His grace. (Hebrews 13:5-6)

Is America and the Church a Spiritual Titanic?
"And they knew not the day of their visitation"
(Luke 19:44)

The *Titanic* analogy for America and the western Church is indeed chilling and undeniable. Just like the ship's crew, we have long been hearing and noting warnings — but making no major changes in foundational spiritual prayer practice! Through much prayerful research, I am convinced we are faced with imminent disaster unless there is major, sustained repentance. Even if God sent no judgment whatsoever, the mere cumulative consequences of societal sin are easily enough to devastate our land! But make no mistake — a holy God must eventually bring judgment upon blatant ongoing sin and severe abomination. (Jeremiah 5:7-9; Galatians 6:9) His holy nature *requires* Him to respond to continuing rebellion. (Jeremiah 5:7-9) If He did not eventually respond, He would be violating His own holy word.

In Luke 19:41, we find Jesus weeping over Jerusalem as they were missing their opportunity to respond to God. America and the Church are almost certainly in a similar position of risk. Indeed, we have received one warning and opportunity after another with little serious repentance. There is great likelihood the door of opportunity may even now be closing.

Mark this well — if there is not a major course correction, the spiritual future of America is dark beyond our ability to comprehend. For the past fifty years, wickedness and family collapse have been increasing rapidly. But now, we are entering an unusual "cumulative convergence" of evil factors from nearly every direction. Conditions of pervasive evil are poised to move from the rapid growth we've seen to exponential explosion!

The Two-Fold Nature of the Spiritual Iceberg
"Sins Laws of Reaping and God's Judgment"

Iceberg Dead Ahead is designed to reveal the size, nature and near certainty of the spiritual and social disaster right in our path. For clarity, let me explain by the term "iceberg," I do not necessarily mean one event (though there will likely be major events.) I refer to a series of events and rapidly escalating conditions of spiritual darkness. Though these are serious statements, Chapters One through Four fully validate their accuracy. And while it is at least possible we may have several more years of relative calm, several indicators make that increasingly unlikely.

Through these pages, I strongly believe God is seeking to full *awaken* His people to imminent devastation if we do not make serious changes. God is seeking to alert us to the profound degree we have ignored His Word, done despite to His grace and violated His holiness. But above all, God is seeking to draw us to Himself in renewed love and repentance! Yet until believers are truly awakened, convicted and broken before God, serious repentance is extremely unlikely. (2 Corinthians 7:10)

We May Have Already Hit Part of the Iceberg!

During the last several months, God has gripped me with a burden and conviction far beyond my words to express. Like others who pray and wait before God, an urgency has exploded greater than anything we have ever known. In growing numbers, there is truly a "weeping between the porch and the altar." (Joel 2:17) *Something huge is coming and God's people are yet dangerously unresponsive and unprepared!* Today's unprecedented "converging" of demographic, geo-political, social and spiritual factors will almost surely produce massive changes. Without a mighty move of God, coming changes will mean profound moral, social and spiritual declines even far worse than those already witnessed.

Indeed, conditions and signs strongly suggest we have already hit at least part of a major spiritual iceberg. We have unquestionably already sustained major damage that will produce more serious consequences in the days ahead. The only question that remains is whether we will experience full judgment and major disaster. That will be decided by how we respond to God's Scriptural injunctions highlighted in this book.

I want to assure readers I am not some wild-eyed "sky is falling" reactionary writer. But based on Scripture and history, anyone should be able to see today's obvious signs. There is truly overwhelming evidence for unprecedented conditions on the near horizon. If there is not a massive spiritual awakening, we likely have little capacity to even imagine the darkness of coming conditions. In Chapters One through Four, I document the fast approaching "iceberg" and ten biblical signs of rising judgments. Even if God did nothing by way of direct judgment, the mere consequences of such severe moral collapse will bring eventual devastation.

However, let me quickly assure readers, the purpose of this book is *not* negative or defeatist! While creating urgency is a vital part of the purpose, instilling strong faith, repentance and hope are far more the goal. Through God's grace, there may yet indeed be hope of a great awakening *if* we embrace very specific steps of biblical repentance. While it is likely too late to avoid all serious consequences, there is perhaps hope to avert total disaster. And even if disaster comes, there is the possibility of great revival to come out of great darkness. God is powerful and His mercy is "higher than the heavens!" (Psalms 103:11; Hebrews 13:8) Even in some of the darkest, most unlikely times God has graced past generations with remarkable revivals. Just before most major American and European awakenings, morals and spiritual vitality were phenomenally low.[6] Yet God awesomely swept the nations back to Himself! But make no mistake — our time for serious repentance and returning is *now!* My purpose is to help believers know exactly *why* and *how* we must immediately return to God. In fact, it is likely we have already hit the spiritual iceberg and the full damage is simply not yet known.

Recapturing the "Relational Foundations" of Revival
Ten Essential Purposes for This Book

Today there are literally hundreds of good books on prayer and revival and I am not trying to recreate that wheel. However through prayerful research and decades of pastoring, I am utterly convinced there are some essential elements largely missing and unaddressed. Restoring these missing elements is absolutely key to walking with God in true evangelism and revival. I call these keys the "relational foundations" and "essential priorities" for empowered Acts 1:8 churches. Because some very key elements are largely missing from today's churches, it is essential that we address these in the pages ahead. To restore missing elements of closeness and power with God, the book is designed around ten purposes.

First, I believe it is urgent for believers to recognize the strong likelihood we are already under advancing stages of God's judgment. I sense God wants readers to understand the full desperation of current and fast approaching conditions. In other words, this book is an urgent alarm and wake-up call to fervently seek the Lord. Until we become truly broken and serious about repentance, real change is extremely unlikely. **Iceberg Dead Ahead** is intended to bring profound brokenness and urgency to God's people. Without urgency, it is all-too easy to continue with "program business as usual." Regarding prayer and repentance, that is exactly what most are still doing. Most are oblivious to the full seriousness of the current position.

Second, the book analyzes exactly *"why" today's moral collapse is so severe.* Until we fully understand *why* we have so declined and departed from God, an effective return is most unlikely. In clear biblical fashion, this tool seeks to outline the essential missing steps of personal and corporate repentance. Readers will especially focus on practical ways to address the reasons for our decline. Indeed, there are certain foundations that are absolutely necessary for great revivals. Using Scripture and history, I outline these key elements and the practical steps to regain them.

Third, *this tool thoroughly explains the missing "relational foundations" that are so utterly essential to joyful intimacy with God and Acts 1:8 power.* Sadly, these foundations are conspicuously missing from the central patterns and priorities of modern churches. They are also largely missing from most ministry and outreach strategies. Until we restore the relational foundations of abiding in Christ's power, we can never 'see Acts 1:8 power. (Acts 1:4; John 15:4-8) Make no mistake — programs, strategies or promotions can never replace the biblical fullness of the Holy Spirit!

What Are the "Relational Foundations?"

By now, readers are probably wondering, "just what are these relational foundations?" Specifically, I am referring to restoring three elements as major priorities and strong sustained emphases. These elements are the very heart of becoming God-focused and Spirit-guided. The relational foundations are: (1) *A strong focus on powerful personal and corporate prayer,* (2) *A strong focus on deep personal and corporate repentance* and (3) *A strong focus on loving united relationships among believers.* These three foundations comprise the very essence of abiding in Christ. In particular, these elements are the essential means of spiritual fullness for individuals and churches. They are like the "spark plugs and gasoline" that provide power to the five church purposes. Without strong prayer patterns, deep cleansing and unified relationships, no person or church can abide in Christ's closeness and power! They are the absolutely essential patterns of knowing, loving and fearing God.

Unless the relational foundations become central, sustained and practiced priorities, *no one* can walk in the fullness and power of the Holy Spirit. The relational foundations form the essential under-girding and power for Acts 1:8 evangelism. Jesus definitively stated, "without abiding in Me, you can do *nothing.*" (John 15:4-5) The relational foundations are the central ways we truly abide in His closeness and power.

In Chapter Five, we examine powerful ways the relational foundations can be infused at the very heart of all we do. At the risk of sounding audacious, I am absolutely convinced the relational foundations *are* the central missing keys! They are the heart of the "abiding factor" so strongly taught by Jesus. (John 15:1-8) When God made these truths clear in my own spirit, He totally revolutionized my life and church.

Recently, God has helped me write the foundations in a form easily understood and incorporated into all we are and do. I cannot even begin to express my excitement at what God will do in all who return to His essential relational patterns of power. These foundations are utterly key to what we have been missing — God's full awesome presence and power in our midst. As we will see, it's not about more programs. It's about deeper relationship with God and one another!

Fourth, leaders and laymen will come to more fully understand the "seven essential priorities" that constitute all New Testament, Great Awakening churches. Unfortunately, most modern churches have stopped with ministry models and patterns that are seriously inadequate for sweeping revival and evangelism. Most congregations stopped with four or five essential priorities when the New Testament definitely portrays seven! Typically, modern churches became over-balanced toward formulas and programs while minimizing fervent prayer, biblical repentance and relational closeness with one another. Make no mistake — these elements are non-negotiables for revival and biblical power. They simply *must* be top priorities of practice!

What are the Essential Church Priorities?

In this book, we focus on restoring the missing biblical priorities by which churches (and individuals) become truly "God-centered" and "Spirit-empowered." In Chapters Five and Six, readers discover simple ways the missing elements can be added to any church ministry model for revival and Acts 1:8 power. Though these essential elements are incredibly powerful, they are not complicated or out of reach. When we add powerful prayer and deep repentance to the basic five purposes, we have what I call the "seven essential priorities" of New Testament churches.

The seven essential priorities are a clear biblical pattern against which all churches can be measured and strengthened. While each church will have uniqueness, all truly biblical churches will strongly emphasize and consistently practice the seven essential priorities. In essence, the seven essential priorities are simply the relational foundations (prayer, repentance and unity) added or incorporated into the five basic church purposes.

If churches continually prioritize deep prayer, repentance and unity, all the other efforts can then have power. *However*, when the first three are marginalized, spiritual power is greatly limited (no matter how hard we try to work the five purposes). For clarity, the seven essential priorities of New Testament, revived churches are as follows: (1) Personal and corporate prayer, (2) Personal and corporate repentance, (3) Fellowship/unity, (4) Evangelism/missions, (5) Discipleship/preaching, (6) Ministry with God's revealed vision and (7) Worship in Spirit and truth. If a congregation consistently focuses on the seven priorities, they will function with God's vision in His power! Whether a church is fully contemporary, traditional or somewhere in the middle, all can learn to experience God's manifest presence through the seven biblical priorities.

Fifth, this tool purposes to restore greater biblical understanding of God's holy nature, His rising judgments and the serious consequences of blatant, persistent sin. We will explore ways to restore saints to a full biblical knowledge of God's nature. (Many have created a false "god" in their own image.) Indeed, how can we return to God if we don't even know Who He is? Surveys leave no doubt that many modern believers have lost the biblical fear and reverence for the Holy God of Scripture. Many seem to think grace means sin has few consequences and that God rarely judges people, churches or nations. Of course, such reasoning is utterly unbiblical and dangerous![8] In fact, today's growing signs of judgment are very clear to those with knowledge of God's corrective patterns in Scripture.

We Are Already Under Advancing Stages of Judgment!

In light of America's tremendous past blessings and protection from God, we now stand at fearsome risk of severe judgment. Not only did we begin as a Christian nation, we have time and again enjoyed God's phenomenal blessings, miraculous victories, protection, merciful preservations and gracious spiritual awakenings. We have also had unequalled exposure to God's Word and truth. These two factors (unusual blessing and high exposure to truth) place America and her churches at unparalleled accountability before God. (Luke 12:47-48)

For America (and many churches) to have so abandoned God and His word, one can only wonder at His grace in having not already brought devastating judgment. In the last fifty years, we have thrown prayer and God's word out of our schools, murdered nearly fifty million unborn babies and exalted perversion as "normal." In the face of all this blasphemy, most churches have remained asleep and shamefully silent. Beyond question, we have horrifically offended God and stand at enormous risk of His righteous judgment. Based on the clear teaching of Scripture and history, America is on borrowed time for serious humbling and judgment. In a teaching series by Avery Willis (author of **Masterlife**) he identified seven scriptural phases of God's increasing judgment.[8] By that outline, America and many churches are *far* down the path to cataclysmic judgment.

In this book, readers will come to realize the serious degree to which many believers and churches have grieved and offended God. A key purpose is to help saints recognize (and avoid) God's judgments while understanding His purposes in trials. Through these pages, we will examine exactly how believers can return to God in good times or bad. It is sobering to realize our generation now has virtually every sign of nations or churches approaching serious judgment. Worse yet, rising signs suggest much worse on the near horizon.

Sixth, we purpose to help believers grasp the nature of true biblical repentance. Unfortunately, many have lost the meaning of biblical repentance.[9] In Chapter Seven, readers will recapture a true understanding and powerful experience of lifestyle repentance. We will clearly outline the necessary steps to repent and avert judgment. The tool also teaches how to seek and walk with God in judgment (should it fall.) Above all, this material is about practical resources for making the essential changes in our experience with God. I need to be clear about the present urgency. Current signs are so serious, we may well have moved into deeper trials before some have even read these pages!

Based on the clear biblical patterns of judgment, we are far down the scale of remedial judgment and are likely very close to a shift into the cataclysmic. Dear saints, it is essential that we "seize the moment" and make powerful foundational changes, not merely adopt some new phrases or re-shuffle strategies. While God may show extended mercies, we must not presume that. In fact given today's conditions, we should presume judgment *is* imminent!

Should we indeed enter into new phases of judgment or trial, Chapter Six contains clear biblical instructions on how God's people are to respond in days of difficulty. Increasingly, Christians are in a type of exile in a pagan land. But remember — God often brings glorious revival out of great trials! Above all, this book is about hope for ultimate repentance and transformation. (No matter what happens in the days ahead.)

Seventh, this journey is about renewed love and surrender to the God we have grieved and profaned by rampant apathy, materialism and sin. Most of all, this tool is about loving obedience, spiritual intimacy and vibrant faith toward our God. Dear saints, our greatest concern should not be that we might face hard times, but that God's holy name has been shamed and His gospel hindered by our spiritual impotence! Though **Iceberg Dead Ahead** is designed to produce deep urgency about the darkness ahead, it is even more to bring a burning passion for returning to God Himself.

We must also understand if God does choose to severely judge and chastise, He is utterly justified and right in doing so! As we examine today's devastating spiritual conditions, we must "make the connection" it is *our* sin that has caused God to withhold His full presence and power.[10] In coming pages, we will see precisely how we have grieved God's Spirit, profaned His name and offended His holy nature. We will also see exactly how we can now return to Him. When it comes to our great and merciful God — hope springs eternal for those that are truly His!

Eighth, this tool is for helping believers experience God's full manifest presence in their lives, families, churches and nation. The goal is to help readers learn how to seek and experience God Himself, not just temporal blessings, earthly comforts or church programs. It is about learning to walk in dynamic prayer, spiritual victory and phenomenal intimacy with Christ. When believers learn to walk in powerful daily prayer and cleansing, their power and growth quickly explode to whole new levels.[11] Once believers truly understand the abiding fullness of His Spirit, all things become possible! As pastors, churches and denominations learn to function under God's full direction and empowerment, ministries explode with an awesome new vibrancy. This tool outlines the essential missing steps to close hearing and walking with God.

Ninth, the book guides believers to Acts 1:8 witnessing and deep heart preparation for Christ's return. In Chapters Six and Seven, readers discover the tools for Acts 1:8 lifestyle witnessing and deep preparation of Christ's Bride. This journey is for experiencing deep personal victory and vibrant Christian living. Rather than just warning about potential catastrophes, the greater goal is spreading Christ's kingdom and preparing saints for the coming wedding of Christ's return! Even as conditions intensify and trials increase, believers can learn to walk in joyful intimacy with Jesus. This tool prepares believers and churches walk in revival no matter what happens in the days ahead.

Tenth, the purpose is raising Joshuas and Calebs to repent and believe God for the next Great Awakening! While we will first take a heart-rending look at current conditions, the ultimate purpose encouraging saints to turn to God in repentance. As readers gaze on the greatness of God, they will receive faith to believe for sweeping revival in our day. Our Lord tells us expectant faith is crucial to releasing His powerful activity. (Mark 11:22; Matthew 17:20) This tool is designed to help believers face today's deepening darkness with overcoming faith and mountain-moving prayer. It leads them to a specific *covenant* of united prayer and repentance. (See

Appendix B for a useable covenant.) When God's people covenant to pray and repent, all things are possible!

What This Book Is *Not*

*This tool is **not** an attack on programs, strategies or innovative methods.* While I clearly highlight today's dramatic decline "in spite of" multiple programs and training, I am in no way demeaning quality methods, promotional strategies or tools. In fact, there is little doubt today's low baptisms and collapsed morals would have been worse without many biblical efforts of faithful leaders.

The problem is usually not so much the programs as a lack of serious prayer and repentance "alongside" them. (Though in some cases, unbalanced programs are indeed a concern.) The central problem is that most are trying to work the programs without deep personal holiness and prayer intimacy with Jesus. Our Lord made this abundantly clear in Acts 1:4 and John 15:4-5. Without the full empowerment of God's Spirit that comes from deep abiding in Jesus, we can do nothing! In this book, we examine the essential ways to recapture true God-focus and biblical balance. Through intense prayer, repentance and spiritual fullness, we can experience the grace of God's awesome manifest presence.[12]

*This resource is **not** presenting some rigid formula or program that "guarantees" revival and change.* While we clearly describe the missing "relational foundations" and "essential priorities" of revived, New Testament churches, these are not rigid programs all churches must practice in exactly the same fashion. Neither am I saying just doing certain acts of repentance will automatically make God work. Our God is awesome and sovereign! While we must surely do our part to repent and seek His face, God will work by His own will and way. (Philippians 2:12-13)

Instead of a rigid formula, this tool contains the essential missing relational principles by which believers and churches can walk in Spirit-empowered intimacy with Christ. Only as believers rediscover true prayer, repentance and fullness, can they begin to experience God's unique vision for each life and congregation. Above all, this tool is about closeness, joyful surrender and New Testament power in Jesus!

*This book is **not** about merely trying to avoid judgment or escape difficult times.* It is truly vital that we get our "motives" right in seeking repentance. The right motives are glorifying God's name, spreading His kingdom and preparing Christ's Bride for His coming![13] We should repent because we love God and want to know and please Him. True repentance comes from a "godly sorrow" that is grieved because we have offended God and broken the love relationship He saved us to experience. (2 Corinthians 7:10) Dear saints, the primary reason we should seek God is the glory of His name and spread of His kingdom in all the earth. If all we're trying to do is "get blessed or avoid problems," our motives are seriously inadequate. (Ezekiel 33:31; James 4:1-4)

As believers, our central motivation is to hallow God's name and spread His kingdom. (Matthew 6:9-10) Far above our own personal desires, we must become burdened that God's name is profaned by rampant sin and weakness in churches. This tool helps increase believers' passion to see God's name hallowed in all the earth. It is also designed to focus our eyes on the awesome power and greatness of the God we serve. When we learn to focus on God, we learn to walk in vibrant faith.

*The book's strong focus on repentance is **not** presented as condemnation or legalism.* In reality, repentance is *positive* not negative! It is accomplished by grace through faith in the fullness of God's empowerment. (Colossians 2:6) While this tool definitely calls for major adjustments and change, it points readers to God's grace for making it possible. Our journey is about the *joy* of repentance and the *power* of true intimacy in Christ, not condemnation or self effort. Rather than being beaten down or discouraged, readers discover how surrender and fullness brings God's power to revolutionize believers and churches.

Our recommended resources strongly emphasize the believer's identity and union in Jesus. Indeed, true repentance is not about condemnation or legalism, but life, power and grace to change through Jesus. While true repentance is certainly about a total change of heart and action, it is even more about knowing, loving and walking close with God. Even in desperately dark times, ours can be a journey of life and hope, not condemnation and despair!

A Personal Word of Balance and Perspective

This book has been among the most difficult yet also easiest of most I have written. It was difficult because of its huge volume of research and the deadly serious message it presents. It was also difficult because of an unusual level of satanic resistance to its completion. In many ways, writing this book has been bloody war. It is quite clear the devil does not want this message to spread among God's people. He very much wants us to "sleep on" and conduct "business as usual." On the other hand, the book was easier than some because of God's overwhelming nearness and strong direction in the writing. Based on Scripture, history and demonstrable facts, I am utterly convinced of the truth, balance and supernatural timing of this urgent word to God's people.

I especially stress that I in no way write as some arrogant judge or critic of others. In fact, it is with deep sorrow that I must chronicle the tragic realities of modern conditions. In several of these points, God has brought profound brokenness, conviction and repentance to my own heart. In many ways, I am writing to myself as much or more than anyone else. Yet this is a book I simply *had* to write at this precise moment in time. Just three months ago, this resource was not even on my radar screen (though the research and truths have been ready for some years.) In very dramatic fashion, I sensed God moved it in front of all the other books I am slated to soon publish. Though I feel most unworthy to write it, the sense of God's timing and urgency has been incredibly strong. A spiritual iceberg is fast approaching!

I have also sensed a special urgency to be extremely balanced in content and focus. Without careful attention, a book of this nature could potentially overstate negative conditions to make a point. Thus, as we examine today's serious signs of decline, it is also important to note the positive signs of God's activity. Indeed, not everything is bad and we should certainly draw hope from what God *is* doing throughout the land. While negative signs of evil are far greater in size and scope, there are definitely some things for which to praise our Lord. For balance, perspective and hope, consider sixteen points of God's present activity.

Not All is Dark!
Sixteen Signs of God's Current Activity

1. Surveys show most Americans still believe in God and have at least some interest in spiritual things.[14] Though this fact is definitely positive, we must acknowledge the interest is often somewhat shallow and self-focused. Unfortunately, significant numbers are essentially trying to re-define God and spirituality in their own image.
2. Some denominations are indeed placing more focus on Acts 1:8 evangelism, missions and church planting (though actual results in the US are still very minimal.) However, there are a few isolated spots of special blessing (i.e. Falls Creek in Oklahoma, encouraging church planting in various states.)

3. A movement of prayer continues to increase and now shows at least some signs of deepening.[15] Significant fasting and prayer are on the rise. A growing number of churches are also returning to corporate prayer meetings. There is even a small movement toward repentance and solemn assembly. Movements like the Global Day of Prayer (from South Africa) have further exploded dramatically.

4. Some denominations have halted a drift toward liberalism and a few others have yet to experience any moves away from Scriptural authority (i.e. Southern and Independent Baptists, Assemblies of God, Conservative Baptists, Churches of God, Bible Fellowships, etc.)

5. A small but growing number of pastors, leaders and laymen are increasingly burdened for evangelism, revival, prayer and repentance. Pastor's prayer groups are definitely increasing.[16]

6. A small but growing number of denominational leaders are to beginning to call churches to seriously repent and seek God's face (i.e. various awakening themes at national denominational meetings and state conventions.)

7. A domestic church planting movement is making progress and among some denominations, missions volunteerism is definitely up.[17]

8. Globally there are powerful evangelism and church planting movements in huge populations like Africa, China and India.[18] A fair number of foreign missionaries report solid numbers of conversions and healthy discipleship.

9. At least some innovative methods and small-group strategies are being blessed (though frankly, others are dangerously unbalanced.) Small group expansion is especially notable as a positive activity of God.

10. We are seeing at least modest sparks of revival at some colleges, universities and seminaries.[19] There are encouraging signs of spirituality in a growing remnant of

young people. A few seminaries are slowly beginning to include some utterly essential emphases that have long been neglected (i.e. teaching on prayer meetings, solemn assemblies, relational unity, God's awesome holiness, judgment, fear of God, etc.)

11. At least some of the worship movement is showing modest signs of increasing its depth and balance. An emphasis on repentance and holiness is slowly increasing.

12. Among some, there is a growing awareness we've tried every strategy and yet are sinking faster than ever. (In other words, there is an increasing readiness to humble ourselves and fervently pray in total dependence on God.) At least some are at last ready to return to the "relational foundations" and "spiritual fullness factor" of abiding in Christ.

13. There is a small praying remnant whose faith is intensifying. Increasingly, they are fasting and receiving definite promises from God. Some states are adopting a major "covenant" to pray for sweeping revival and spiritual awakening. (See Appendix B) We should find hope in the fact past sweeping awakenings came from small praying remnants of dedicated saints (not huge numbers.)

14. Americans still send many missionaries and much benevolent help to people around the world.

15. America still basically supports and defends Israel against hostile forces. (Though that support has lessened and some politicians on the horizon would abandon them in a heartbeat.)

16. In spite of America's severe moral collapse and overall church weakness, evidences of God's protective mercies are to some degree still present. While we definitely see strong evidence of lessening protection, at least "some" shielding is still in place. (Though that could easily change in a single day.)

Yet Evil Trends *Far* Overwhelm the Positives

After reading the sixteen encouraging signs, some may even believe the "tide has turned" and revival is at hand. Today some even declare we are already in revival. Unfortunately, that sentiment shows no understanding of the awesome societal impact of past historic awakenings. We are seeing little that even begins to compare with God's phenomenal movement in past awakenings. While it is encouraging to see God is definitely at work, every reader needs to understand a most crucial reality. "In spite of the various positives, the evil trends are as yet *far* greater in size, intensity and growth!"

At current rates, we are fast losing America. In fact, we have in many ways already lost it! None of today's positives have prevented today's ever worsening moral and spiritual collapse. At present, positive indicators are hardly even putting a dent in today's low baptisms, church declines or horrific moral and family collapse. Tragically, overall moral conditions and values are getting much worse! Strong evidence also reveals a "cumulative effect" likely to exponentially worsen several of the evil trends.

Yet some wonder if perhaps God could somehow just sweep in and change everything in a heart beat. Yes, He really could do that and it might yet happen. In past awakenings there were often points where there was a miraculous "suddenness" of God awesome manifest presence. (Acts 2:2, 43) When God "rends the heavens," suddenly the whole atmosphere is spiritually charged with His holy presence.[20] Based on patterns in several past awakenings, a true revival could mean *twenty to thirty million* Americans saved and joining churches in just the next three to five years! Believers, our hope and prayer must ever be for just such a merciful and miraculous move of God's presence.

However, Scripture and history are clear that God sovereignly moves mostly as His people respond to His grace in deep brokenness, prayer and repentance. In James 4:8-10 He says it plainly. *"Draw near to God and He will draw near to you. Cleanse your hands, you sinners; and purify your hearts, you double-minded. Lament and mourn and weep! Let your laughter be turned to mourning and your joy to gloom. Humble yourselves in the sight of the Lord and He will lift you up."* While the power is all of God's grace, He clearly tells us to seek Him in serious repentance.

In the Greek text, the word for cleanse and purify (*katharizō*) is definitely not referring to shallow, surface confession. As used in this context, the words surely mean deep cleansing with full repentance. "Mourning and weeping" certainly do not accompany brief, shallow confession. (James 4:9) Dear saints, it is vital that we fully grasp the urgency of embracing much deeper steps of humility, repentance and prayer. While revival is all of God's grace, He requires us to choose serious prayer and repentance. (2 Chronicles 7:14; Philippians 2:12-13; James 4:8-10) *Only* as we recapture the missing relational foundations can we again see God's mighty hand in glorious, nation-shaking power!

Understanding What is at Stake
Recognizing Our Crucial "Moment of Visitation"
(Luke 19:44)

Based on fast escalating changes, we likely have very little time before far greater darkness engulfs society. To those who understand biblical patterns, warnings of potential judgments are sounding with deafening urgency. Make no mistake — *now* is our crucial moment! Just as Israel slept through their crucial moment of "visitation" (or opportunity), we are in profound danger of doing the same thing regarding repentance and revival. The next five to ten years are absolutely crucial to whether we will experience God in revival or serious judgment. It is almost certainly going to be one or the other! Just rocking along is no longer an option if we are to have any hope of revival. As opposition and trials increase, the days of "casual Christianity" are quickly coming to an end. *We must immediately return to God in major repentance or prepare to live under serious persecution, trials and judgment!*

It is urgent that readers truly know what is at stake. Above all, the glory of God's name and spread of His gospel are at state! We should be broken because His glorious name and gospel have been profaned and hindered by our gross spiritual weaknesses. It is also vital that we consider the futures of our children and grandchildren. In reality, some of us (because of age) will likely die before things turn truly catastrophic. It is almost like the Titanic analogy when women and children got into the life boats and the men drowned. But this time it will be tragically reversed. Today it is likely our children and grandchildren (not older adults) that will face the full horror if we fail to turn our spiritual ship.

So what about your children and grandchildren? Will their generations look back at us and say, "how could they have continued with programs as usual while a massive spiritual iceberg loomed dead in their path? How could they have remained complacent in the face of so many signs and warnings? Indeed, why did they keep following the same basic patterns though they were clearly not working? Why did they slide into total collapse with little or no serious calls to fervent prayer and solemn assembly? How could their leaders not sound the alarms and declare full spiritual emergency?"

So how about it believers? How *do* we answer those questions? Yet there may be a glimmer of light. At this point, perhaps we could perhaps still repent and those heart-rending questions might never be asked! In light of today's conditions, failure to change is like a subtle form of spiritual insanity. Think about it — does it really make any sense to continue the same or similar patterns that have ushered in the worst spiritual collapse in American history? It makes no sense at all!

A Definition of Spiritual Insanity
"Doing the Same Things but Expecting Different Results"

During today's fifty year baptism decline and moral collapse, churches have essentially repeated similar approaches with periodic efforts at strategy revision. While we change slogans and tweak the focus, most modern approaches still marginalize intense prayer, repentance and abiding in Jesus. The foundational patterns of fervent prayer, holiness and spiritual fullness have simply not been highly prioritized. In reality, our approach has largely been "push harder, peddle faster, program smarter and promote louder." While all of these activities *certainly* need to be done, they are obviously not the central answer!

One thing is certain — it is fervent prayer, spiritual intimacy, heart passion and the resulting "power" we lack, *not* methodology. Tragically, we have mostly maintained the same predominant focus on new programs and promotions. At the same time, we mostly marginalized the relational foundations of intense prayer, deep repentance and Christian unity. Without meaning too, many indeed committed the irrational and fatal error — we continued the same basic patterns but expected different results! Current conditions leave no doubt as to the sad result. Surely we cannot expect major changes by following the same basic patterns that allowed (and caused) today's unprecedented collapse! This book is about recognizing and embracing the missing steps of repentance and change.

A Special Word to Church and Denominational Leaders
It's Time to Tell Our People the "Full Truth"

Dear pastors and leaders, *you* are the absolute key to whether our spiritual ship turns in time. And even if the nation does not see sweeping revival, perhaps your family, church or denomination could! In Appendices C and D, I list biblical steps for change and helpful resources. As you reflect on these vital missing steps, please don't sell your people short. Though this book is not a shallow read, neither is it complicated. I urge you to have your entire congregation (agency or denomination) thoroughly read these pages. It is high time that we fully expose our people to something beside the ABC's of spiritual basics. We must tell believers the full truth of our real condition. It is essential that we guide them into the necessary steps for repentance. If you encourage and guide them, they can certainly grasp (and be deeply moved) by the realities and truths in this tool.

The reason for church-wide distribution and promotion is simple. Once believers truly understand the urgency, they will desire the specific changes you present. However, if they don't fully understand the *how* and *why* of major adjustments, they will not follow with their hearts and may well resist your leadership. It is absolutely *imperative* that God's people are awakened to true conditions and to God's specific paths of repentance. As leaders, our greatest responsibility is to tell people the truth, not rock them to sleep. It is *unspeakably urgent* that we now awaken God's people to today's serious realities and the necessary steps of repentance!

Let me also stress this book is published in a non-profit fashion. There is no financial motive in urging great numbers to read it. It is my belief the subject is too holy and urgent to be sullied by the high profit mark-up that accompanies far too many modern resources. I do not want there to be any barriers to whole churches receiving this message. Thousands of copies will also be donated to other countries. Even in countries currently in revival, the tool is prayerfully presented as a "preventative measure." It is designed to help prevent their drifting down the same paths that have caused our severe spiritual decline. Indeed, other countries can learn much from our experience. They can learn the tragic consequences of high programming, low prayer and little spiritual cleansing.

As we turn our eyes to the path ahead, the purpose is to fully analyze the spiritual "iceberg" of fast developing conditions. In Chapters One through Three, I believe God will convince saints we *must* make foundational changes in our priorities of prayer, repentance, unity and spiritual fullness. I especially pray the next chapters will help us fully comprehend the futility of seeking different results by new slogans, faster pedaling or tweaked strategies alone. It is essential that we now become broken, humble and wise enough to come back to Jesus' non-negotiable truth of abiding in His fullness and power. *"My house shall be called a house of prayer .... wait for the promise of the Father..... unless you abide in Me, you can do nothing."* (Matthew 21:13; Acts 1:4; John 15:5) Indeed, these are the essential relational foundations of Acts 1:8 power!

Understanding Your Journey Through This Book

As readers prepare to pray through this book, it will help to understand the flow and path of the journey. Chapters One through Three fully describe the vast size and worsening nature of the iceberg ahead. The first three chapters help believers grasp our true condition and exactly *why* we came to this desperate point of crisis. Saints, if we don't know our true position and how we got here, there is little chance of major change. If we don't fully understand the real possibility of imminent judgment and destruction, we are not likely to repent! In the first four chapters, you will receive a God-given brokenness and urgency regarding our homes, churches and nation. As did Nehemiah, we must thoroughly survey our true spiritual condition and weep before the God of heaven. (Nehemiah 1:4)

Yet as God grips your heart with deep urgency, do not be overwhelmed! In Appendices C and D, I list practical ways we *can* return to God in revival. The steps are very practical and newly available resources make powerful changes possible for any congregation or group. Once Nehemiah saw the desperate need, He also looked to the greatness of God's mercy and power. Remember saints — we serve a big God who can still "rend the heavens." Our great Savior can shake nations with one breath of His mighty Holy Spirit!

A "United Covenant" of Prayer and Repentance
Raising Up Nehemiahs, Joshuas and Calebs for Today!

Ultimately, this book is a strong call to specific action for turning our spiritual ship. My fervent desire is to see God quicken the hearts of millions with a burning desire to see things change! To God's praise, there *are* things we can do. In Appendix B, readers are equipped to embrace a very specific "Covenant of Prayer and Repentance." It contains focused biblical prayers for revival, evangelism and deep personal repentance. Believers are asked to embrace them (or similar) prayers in their personal quiet times, church prayer meetings and denominational agencies. By so doing, we utilize the awesome power of praying in agreement according to the will of God. (Matthew 18:19; 1 John 5:14-15) If millions of believers truly unite in prayer and repentance, we already know the outcome! *"If My people who are called by My name will humble themselves, and pray and seek My face, and turn from their wicked ways, then I will hear from heaven, and will forgive their sin and heal their land."* (2 Chronicles 7:14)

Dear readers, God wants to fill saints with the bold faith of Joshua and Caleb. When faced with impossible odds, they said "we can take the land" and "give me this mountain." (Numbers 14:8; Joshua 14:12) my prayer is that God will use these pages to awaken a million new Joshuas and Calebs! Let us all remember the glorious invitation of God in Psalms 2:8. *"Ask of Me and I will give you the nations for your inheritance."* May we be inspired by earlier saints like Evan Roberts who believed God and saw whole nations transformed in sweeping revival (i.e. Wales in 1904.)[17] Though the hour is dark, we must focus on the mighty God who has shaken dark nations time and time again. Saints, our Lord has *not* lost His power — let us *not* lose our faith! (Hebrews 12:1-2; 13:8)

A Prayer For Every Reader

"Lord, open my eyes to Your awesome glory and holiness — Show me our real condition and break my heart for the offense our sin and weakness have brought to Your name — Help me understand my need for deep spiritual intimacy, fervent prayer and genuine fullness of the Holy Spirit — Teach me the futility of conducting churches, programs and strategies without Your awesome manifest presence. — Help me understand my need of Your fullness for daily victory and for loving my family. — Gracious Father, grant me a repentant heart, clear understanding and the revelation faith to believe for the next Great Awakening. — Fill me with a burning love for You and for souls. — Lord, may You alone be praised. Let Your kingdom come on earth as it is in heaven. "Even so, come Lord Jesus!" (Revelation 22:20)

A Sobering Look at the Iceberg

"Thirty One Signs of Spiritual Desperation and Rising Judgments"

A Time to Weep Over Broken Spiritual Walls!

"The wall of Jerusalem is also broken down, and its gates are burned with fire." *So it was, when I heard these words, that **I sat down and wept, and mourned for many days; I was fasting and praying before the God of heaven**."* (Nehemiah 1:3d-4)

Chapter One

Signs of Moral and Social Desperation
"Recognizing the Signs of Fast Rising Judgment"
(Signs 1-7)

To stir our hearts to seek God, we now fully consider the disturbing signs of today's conditions. In these chapters, we will do exactly what Nehemiah did in his day. (Nehemiah 1:2-3) We will thoroughly survey the true spiritual condition of our cities, homes, churches and denominations. At points in this section, some may wonder if I am exaggerating the severity of today's spiritual conditions. Readers should understand that with many factors, I am actually somewhat conservative in the assessment. With most statistics, my methodology was to average several different surveys and present figures somewhere between the high and low extremes. So many wild figures get tossed around I resolved to use the more middle ranges. If anything, conditions are even worse and I could have included several additional signs of concern.

In these chapters, others may wonder if perhaps I am ignoring or downplaying various signs of progress and hope. Believe me, I in no way delight in outlining these disturbing truths. With all my heart, I wish I could share a different set of facts. Yet, the only way I could is to ignore God's Word and the current signs exploding from every direction. Frankly, it would be easier to keep our heads buried in the sand, keep pushing programs and just "hope it will all work out." Yet the certain result of such an approach is betrayal to God, to our children and the eventual destruction of society. The facts revealed in the next chapters strongly suggest we are already under advancing stages of judgment that could well turn cataclysmic (if we don't repent!)

Assessing What Has Occurred On Our Spiritual Watch
Understanding Our Enormous Risk of Judgment

Please know I have thoroughly examined the various "good" signs often touted as hopeful indicators of potential growth and renewal. While there definitely are "some" positive signs, I again stress most do not even begin to off-set the rising tidal wave of negatives. It is also true that several of the "so-called" positive signs tend to collapse under careful biblical analysis and honest projection. They're not enough to even begin to turn the tide. Tragically, some things now proclaimed as "hopeful" are neither "balanced" nor "New Testament." Furthermore, when you analyze "actual results," nothing we are seeing is keeping pace with the explosion of evil. At present, today's negative signs seriously overwhelm any hopeful indicators. Saints, we are utterly desperate for nothing less than another historic Great Awakening. Indeed, we are *far* past mercy drops being of much real help.

And now as did Nehemiah, we begin by taking a long hard look at current conditions. We must become fully honest about the developments on our "spiritual watch." Yet as Nehemiah, let us remember *faith* and *hope* in our brokenness! But make no mistake — the hour is unspeakably urgent. There really is an "iceberg dead ahead!" It is time to be broken and mourn for God's Name and for a nation plunging away from God. May God now move us to the brokenness, prayer and repentance today's conditions truly warrant.

Thirty-One Signs of Desperation and Judgment
"A Sobering Look At Broken Down Walls"
(Nehemiah 1:3)

1. Over the last forty years, biblical morality, marriage patterns and family strength have not merely declined, they have witnessed an

> *unprecedented collapse.[21] Worse yet, this unprecedented collapse has now permeated deep into modern churches.[22]*

As disturbing as is today's moral collapse, it is most troubling to see how deeply it has saturated so many believers and churches. Tragically, today's devastating modern decline has deeply permeated believers and churches. To our utter shame, today's catastrophic divorce rates are actually worse in the Bible belt![23] Under our spiritual watch, we have witnessed at least a *five-fold* explosion of people living together outside of wedlock.[24] Any slight improvement in some regions' divorce rates are almost certainly because such vast numbers no longer even bother to get married.[25] When that factor is fully considered, there are few (if any) actual glimmers of light in today's catastrophic moral and family collapse.

It is important to realize, today's decimation of family strength is utterly unprecedented in national history. We are now even witnessing growing efforts to re-define the very meaning of marriage. Anti-family laws and proposals laughable just ten years ago are now under serious discussion with steadily increasing public acceptance. In fact, the population percentages that hold a biblical family view are steadily eroding. And make no mistake — when the foundations are destroyed, that society is *given over* to vilest depravity. (Psalms 11:3; Romans 1:20-32)

Christian leaders, in light of today's devastating collapse, how could we have any attitude but utter brokenness and desperate seeking after God? Absolutely nothing in modern experience warrants the slightest degree of over-confidence in today's programs, promotions and techniques. Current conditions demand that we stop and seriously ask what elements are missing in our churches compared to earlier generations. We obviously don't just need a little better programming or promotion. Dear saint, do you see the signs of the times? What time it is spiritually? It is time for a complete return to the missing "relational foundations" of fervent prayer, deep repentance and unity with one another! It is time to return to the true and living *God* (not some shallow creation of our own imaginations.) Only a serious return to the relational foundations will release the fullness of God's Spirit through our lives.

> 2. *Reverential fear of God, respect for Christ's Church, belief in the Bible and regard for Christians has plummeted to shockingly low levels. Vast percentages no longer have any real sense of sins' accountability to the holy God Who judges all wickedness. They fear neither sin's consequences nor God's righteousness judgment.*

Throughout all history, it is extremely rare to see societal respect for God and morality collapse so much in such a small amount of time. In fact, it may well be unprecedented. Today, the reverential fear of God and Scripture have dramatically declined in many of the nation's churches! In society at large, irreverence has become even far worse. Overwhelming multitudes now completely reflect the tragic conditions described in Psalms 36:1. *"There is no fear of God before his eyes."* By the way, this condition is strongly suggestive of a nation "given over" to its own utter depravity. (Romans 1:20-30)

Current patterns reflect an unmitigated collapse of reverence for God and belief in the literal truth of Scripture. In just one generation, Christians have gone from having fairly strong public esteem to being virtually the only group it is fashionable to slander and mock. God's holy name is now regularly profaned and mocked from nearly every public forum. Godless actors, comedians, professors and talk show hosts publicly blaspheme Christ in ways they would never dreamed of doing only one generation earlier.

Modern cults and false religions often receive more media respect than biblical Christianity. People who seriously believe in biblical authority and Christian values are now viewed as the "fringe radical right." Not so long ago they were the undisputed center of society. In times of Christian oppression, societies went through certain very predictable patterns that led to overt persecution. The patterns described under this point reveal a nation fast moving down that path. According to Scripture, such a nation is on a collision course with catastrophe and judgment. (Proverbs 14:34) These patterns unquestionably describe a Church in which God's full power and presence is severely withheld. When the Church no longer fears God, society no longer respects or listens to the Church. Believers, what time is it? It is time to return to the reverential fear of the holy God of Scripture! (Not a false creation of a shallow self-seeking society.)

3. *In just one generation evil has not simply increased, it has become "many times" more brazen, blasphemous, perverted and accepted! Both the phenomenal speed and totality of today's collapse is most unusual in Christian history. What we are seeing is not a typical spiritual downturn. It is a full-blown "values reversal" in which good is viewed as evil and evil as good!*

The current generation is unquestionably witnessing something far worse than a cyclical moral downturn. America has now experienced an unprecedented "values reversal." A values reversal is when "good is actually viewed as evil and evil as good." (Isaiah 5:20) Evil and perversion have now sunk to such twisted thinking as to rival the Nazis who slaughtered millions of innocents simply because they were "inconvenient" to the society they wanted.

Since our own nation's so-called great social "enlightenment" and "advancement," we have now slaughtered nearly fifty million unborn babies. And what was their crime? They were simply unwanted or inconvenient![26] (How can God *not* judge our land?) Today the nation's conscience has become so twisted, it has taken bloody political war just to get something as sick and heinous as "partial birth murder" to be halted by the slimmest of margins. ("Partial birth murder" is indeed the only accurate way to describe this vile act.) Yet astoundingly, passionate supporters of this outrage are regrouping by the millions. It is truly shocking to see the degree to which consciences can become perverted, seared and warped. Could there ever be a more appalling example of "evil being viewed as good?"

We increasingly bear a disturbing likeness to Paul's description of a society "given over" to the widespread normalization of grossest depravity and perversion. A society being "given-over" is unquestionably in an advanced stage of judgment. (Romans 1:20-30) And all of this in a land full of churches and Christian programs! In the midst of all our elaborate "programs, prayer promotions, training and innovative methods," something is clearly still missing from modern approaches. It is time to weep for widespread powerlessness to impact society. Through God's manifest presence, the early church shook their society. With all the strategies and strengths, we have essentially lost ours. What time is it? It is time to fervently seek God for the power that only comes from utterly yielded, prayer-filled hearts! This book is about helping individuals and churches return to God-seeking prayer and repentance.

4. *Television, movies and the Internet have exploded pornography and perversion far beyond anything*

> *we could have even imagined just ten years ago.*[27]
> *In all history, there has not been anything like
> today's pervasive media totally saturating society
> with moral and spiritual filth. No propaganda
> machine in history has ever equaled modern
> media.*[28]

In an incredibly short time period, this rushing river of filth has not merely increased, it has exploded exponentially. Literally millions of people are now virtually addicted to pornography (who had not even viewed it just ten years prior!) Surveys show disturbing numbers of clergy and spiritual leaders have viewed Internet pornography.[29] I know of many Christian youth leaders who acknowledge virtually *all* of their male students admit to an ongoing struggle with viewing pornography. Furthermore, today's pornography has gone far past typical sex. It is now filled with grossest perversion, child pornography, bestiality and child rape. In just a few short years, this spiritual scourge has exploded into a raging epidemic.

On the entertainment front, Hollywood is able to flourish only because so many believers think nothing of going to an "R" rated movie because "it has a clever story-line or good actors." According to a recent study (UCLA, 2007), of all the PG-13 rated films from among the 100 top-grossing movies of 1999 and 2000, violence permeated nearly 90 percent of the films studied.[30] Furthermore, what would have been rated R just ten years ago is now PG-13 and on prime time television! (If most Christians seriously boycotted questionable movies, standards would have likely changed long ago.)

Gambling has also exploded with an unprecedented wave of exponential expansion.[31] In state after state, churches have proven powerless to hardly even check (much less stop) this sweeping wave of evil. On this issue, people who call themselves Christians do elaborate moral gymnastics and absurd rationalizations to convince themselves such an obviously wicked vice is somehow "good for society."

Our generation has further witnessed an unprecedented explosive proliferation of witchcraft, psychics, new-ageism, astrology and crime by the very young. It is most disturbing that violent crime is now rising rapidly among two new segments of society — women and young children![32] We have even watched our nation lose the will to enforce its own national borders. Historically, several of the above patterns typically denote a society in advanced stages of moral and social collapse. So what time is it spiritually? It is time to recognize God's judgment and humble ourselves in deep contrition! Believers, we simply do not have time for several more years of "church programs and patterns as usual."

5. *In a remarkably short time period, America has witnessed a massive, unprecedented cultural shift away from a Judeo-Christian world-view and biblical values.[33] It is rare to have ever seen societal attitudes and beliefs decline so much so fast. To move from the America of the 1950's to today's conditions is virtually unwitnessed in history.*

With astounding speed, moral and religious relativism have become the predominate mindset of many Americans and almost all Europeans. In just two generations, the percentages of those who hold a biblical world-view have absolutely plummeted.[34] It is sobering to realize we have the terrible distinction of being the generation of churches and leaders that have presided over America's lightning fast move from a Christian to a post-Christian society.

So what should be our attitude since history's most appalling moral collapse has happened on our spiritual watch? The attitude should be one of profound brokenness, humility, weeping and contrition. If any generation ever needed to put on "sackcloth and ashes," surely it is ours! Dear saints, have we indeed forgotten how to weep? Are our consciences numbed and seared to the point we can no longer be ashamed? (Jeremiah 6:15) We must immediately call ourselves into the most desperate levels of prayer, fasting and repentance. One thing is certain — boasting, swagger and self-confidence should have no place in our attitudes or gatherings. (Yet sadly, they often still do.) It is time to humble ourselves and pray in deep fervency and repentance!

> **Author's Note:** Under the next two points, statements regarding less biblical values of younger generations are not meant as critical or demeaning of younger age groups as a whole. In fact, an exciting renewal is now occurring in a small remnant of younger age blocks! Movements of fervent prayer and repentance are growing in a remnant of committed students. While it is statistically true younger groups have a significantly less biblical world-view and diminished church involvement, it is also true the next revival may well come from the younger generation. We must humbly acknowledge today's devastating spiritual conditions actually developed under the leadership of older generations. In other words, there is plenty of culpability for all age groups. Yet to analyze coming trends, we must make an honest assessment of the beliefs and practice of those "soon to be" decision-makers and leaders for society.

6.   *As the more biblically oriented senior adult voters now rapidly die-off, America is on the verge of a major negative shift in the morality, world-view and personal values of voters who elect government and set policies. Without a massive spiritual awakening, the morality of tomorrow's government and laws*

will bear little resemblance to the America we have known.

Studies clearly show teens and young adults have significantly different morals and world-views than older adults.[35] (Unfortunately, this is also true of disturbingly high numbers who are children of evangelicals.) David Kinnaman in response to a 2007 national study on American beliefs, said the following:

> "Still, a shift away from biblical perspectives are likely to result in significant alternations to the spiritual landscape since a person's beliefs dictates a great deal about their behavior and allegiance." [36]

Studies show alarming numbers of evangelical children abandon church upon reaching young adulthood. Most surveys put the percentage at somewhere between 66-80 percent! [37]

As large numbers from older voting blocks quickly pass away and younger groups fill voting booths, it will become harder and harder to elect anyone with even a semblance of biblical values. (In fact, we may even now be passing the point of critical mass.) Unless God intervenes, these changes will have profoundly negative effects on the laws, judicial courts and spiritual climate of the nation. Over time, the government may well be telling churches which parts of the Bible they can or cannot teach. In a society of such collapsed moral foundations, serious oppression of Christians is not merely possible, it is a virtual certainty. *"What can the righteous do when the foundations are destroyed?"* (Psalms 11:3) In some western nations, it is even now a serious crime to teach certain foundational moral texts from Scripture (e.g. Canada' laws against teaching of passages regarding homosexuality.) Strong forces in America are making relentless strides in the very same directions. Saints, it is time to wake up and fully face the "signs of the times." Without a huge spiritual awakening, radical (and devastating) changes are in our future.

7. *Large percentages of the Mosaic and Baby Buster generations are profoundly impacted by education, music and entertainment industries that are overwhelmingly anti-moral and anti-Christ.*[38] *Consequently, their attitudes, beliefs and values are markedly different than the older age groups (that are now so rapidly dying off.) The profoundly negative impact on attitudes and beliefs is growing with alarming speed.*

Never in history have the forces of secular education, media, music and entertainment been so blatantly and persuasively aligned against God and biblical truth.[39] It is most significant that today's atmosphere is not just *immoral*, it is strongly *anti-Christian*. Profoundly evil, anti-Christ messages daily bombard our society from every conceivable direction. No doubt the deadliest of evils are directed at the impressionable minds of children, youth and young adults.

Many of the nation's schools and universities have a blatant, almost militant bias toward a far more secularized, non-Christian, socialistic society. In disturbing numbers of schools and universities, there are pervasive elements of an anti-American, church bashing, history revising mind-set. Our nation's Christian foundations are now being systematically ignored and (in many cases) blatantly maligned and distorted.[40] The people who set those policies and write such books have no hesitation to blatantly alter or ignore our strong Christian heritage. With people of that character and mindset, truthful scholarship has long since been abandoned. While of course not all schools follow such patterns, troubling numbers do. Consequently, huge percentages of the nation's young are being filled with ideas profoundly destructive to morality, Christian belief and sound judgment concerning history and current world realities.

Incredibly powerful attitude-shaping forces within media and education are fast driving society away from the biblical values and principles that made America great. This is profoundly serious because whoever (or whatever) controls the minds of a nation's young, soon controls the nation! It is hard to even imagine the mindset and values of future adults now being raised in today's spiritually poisonous atmosphere. Many will have been thoroughly brainwashed and conditioned against Christ and Scripture. As seniors quickly pass on, we will almost surely move into a period of even far more radical social and spiritual decline (unless there is an historic Great Awakening.)

Readers should understand the deadly fruit of these conditions are only now "beginning" to become fully manifest. Like a snowball rolling down a hill, the impact will soon become "exponential" in its pervasive effect. There is little question we are fast moving toward just such a cycle. Once a society has been thoroughly de-Christianized, the difficulty of ever seeing it reverse becomes enormous. If you doubt this, just take a look at modern Europe! Saints, unless there is a massive move of God, we haven't seen anything yet. So again I ask, "What time is it?" It is time to seek the Lord with an intensity far greater than current levels. We must call solemn assemblies for seeking God with all our hearts! (Joel 2:12-17) Furthermore, the assemblies must be about truly seeking God, not just a selfish effort to get out of trouble. (Ezekiel 33:31)

Looking Beyond Symptoms to the Cause
"Lukewarm, Powerless and Worldly Churches"

Having examined seven devastating signs in general societal morals, we must now turn attention to the realm of churches and religion. Just as today's moral collapse is unprecedented, so too is the condition of most modern churches and denominations. Of all the possible signs of spiritual desperation and judgment, surely the most telling is among the people of God. It is the condition of the *Church* (not the lost) that most determines blessing or judgment on our land. (2 Chronicles 7:14) In Chapter Three, I fully chronicle the disturbing changes now raging through many churches and denominations. We will also examine significant questions about some of the so-called "good signs" touted by some as evidence of projected church growth and progress. With some of today's church growth theories, there are profound concerns about biblical balance, spiritual depth and long-term fruit.

Saints, it is paramount to realize the condition of churches largely explains the current moral decline. Let us soberly remember the following spiritual truth. *"As go a nation's churches — so goes the nation!* May God give us the honesty to realize America's condition is a direct reflection of it churches. With churches on virtually every corner, only an appalling weakness can explain such a complete and total collapse. If even ten percent of our churches had functioned in true New Testament power, we would have long since seen a Great Awakening. That reality should drive us to deepest brokenness and determination to seek God's face. After all, even today's disgusting moral swamp is not too much for His awesome power! I urge every reader to pause and ask God for a heart to hear His voice to the churches.

Chapter Two

Signs of Desperation and Judgment in Churches and Strategies
(Signs 8-21)

While there are certainly a few notable exceptions, the vast majority of American churches are in significant stages of weakness and decline. Overall baptism ratios have seldom been lower, bickering higher or apathy more pervasive. Even today's more "successful" congregations typically bear little resemblance to the powerful patterns of New Testament or Great Awakening churches. As little as five years ago, I could not accurately say conditions had "never" been worse (because things have been really bad before). Yet in the last five years, we have blown past every previous American generation in levels of moral collapse! Spiritual conditions have reached an unparalleled urgency that is rapidly worsening.

It is indeed important to understand just how unusual today's conditions really are. While things have been horrifically bad before, current conditions are truly unprecedented in depth, severity and comprehensiveness! Yet I again urge readers to remember faith and hope in the greatness of God. Though the current collapse is catastrophic and pervasive, do not give in to despair. Our gracious Lord has provided clear steps for change. As today's conditions move you to brokenness, let them also produce a burning determination to believe God and seek His face. Remember, in Chapters Six and Seven, we will examine very clear steps for repentance and change. As bad as things are, God could certainly reverse the tide if we fully return to Him.

Signs Within Churches and Religion

8. *A large majority of churches and denominations are about to be hit by a huge demographic "age bomb." American churches have never experienced such a dramatic loss of a single age group that comprises so much congregational leadership and financial support. Without a massive spiritual awakening, the soon coming demographic shift will severely impact church attendance, financial support, missions and congregational leadership.*

Many churches are already beginning to feel strong effects of a growing social age-group shift.[41] The effects are just beginning to hit. Soon they will become devastating unless there is a massive spiritual awakening. To illustrate the coming age bomb phenomena, consider what would happen if next Sunday everyone over age 60 was suddenly permanently missing from American churches. It is conservatively estimated that 25-30% of churches would all but disappear! With the level of missing senior attendees, financial givers and workers, it would be virtually impossible to keep these churches open. Another 35-40% of churches would still function but with significantly less attendance, financial strength, leadership, ministry and missions support.[42] (See author's note below.) Their giving, ministries and missions would feel major impact. Only twenty to thirty percent of churches would not be significantly affected.

Recently, I had a most sobering "reality moment" when I led a season of prayer at the national convention of a large denomination. First, I noticed the numbers in attendance were only about one-fourth of attendance levels of twenty-five years ago. (Though controversy made earlier figures higher than normal.) What really got my attention was the number of senior adults that made up such a significant percentage of the attendance. While convention attendance is not always a central measure of denominations, it is indicative of a major shift in demographics and support.

> **Author's Note**: The projected figures of age group losses are an average from many denominations, not just one. While these figures will prove generally true for most, in a few denominations there will be significant variance. A few will be significantly better or worse. But make no mistake — the age bomb will have very significant overall national impact.

A Sobering Exercise and Reality Check

The following exercise will provide a sobering window into the near future. The next time you attend a general association, state or national denomination meeting, take a good look at the age of the crowd and consider the effect if all senior adults were suddenly missing. Try this same exercise in your own church services. For many, these exercises will prove extremely eye-opening and troubling. But unless there is a massive Great Awakening, you are looking at a picture of the not too distant future. Obviously, such changes will have a devastating effect on local churches, denominational entities, evangelism, seminaries and missions support.

Though the age bomb scenario will not explode next Sunday, it will almost certainly manifest as millions of faithful seniors die over the next 10-20 years! This is especially alarming since most in the younger generations in no way match the attendance consistency, financial commitment, family strength, reliable service or church loyalty of their more senior counter-parts.[43] Since millions of the most faithful attendees, leaders and financial supporters are now beginning to rapidly die, the age bomb is not merely a possibility — it is a virtual certainty! After all, people are not suddenly going to start living to be 120 years old! Only a huge, heaven-sent awakening can off-set the severe effects of this fast approaching wave of losses. As bad as is the spiritual situation in America, conditions are many times worse in Europe.

Without a miraculous influx of faithful, new members from younger ages, we are rapidly approaching major losses in church attendance and giving. It is extremely sobering to consider what such loses will do to denominational, seminary and missions support. If we are going to avert this serious future impact to God's work, we must embrace major spiritual changes *now*. The next five to ten years are absolutely crucial! We must make foundational spiritual adjustments, not just a few new slogans or strategy adjustments. The age-bomb alone is truly a massive "iceberg dead ahead!" Unfortunately, there are many looming factors besides the massive loss of senior members.

Whether or not we yet realize it, we *are* desperate for another historic explosion of God's manifest presence. And what brings such mighty explosions of revival? Throughout Scripture and history, the answer never varies. *Only* far deeper levels of contrition, prayer, repentance and fasting can reverse today's exploding tide of evil! As we consider the coming age bomb and desperate need for revival, it is also vital to take an honest look at current patterns of evangelistic impact on unchurched society.

A Crucial Perspective on Analyzing Evangelistic Impact

Before addressing the next two points, let me stress that the following observations are in no way meant to demean biblical soul winning promotions, evangelistic events or area-wide outreach strategies. *Indeed, we must always heavily promote solid evangelism and gospel seed sowing!* In fact, it is this author's strong opinion they should be promoted even far more. (Though I stress they must be true gospel presentations, not shallow incomplete counterfeits.)

Beyond question, those who help us witness and sow seeds are among the bright spots of each generation! Were it not for their faithful efforts and tools, today's low baptisms would have likely been even lower. We should *always* praise God for truly biblical efforts at evangelism, gospel saturation and seed sowing. The problem may *not* so much be the strategies as it is a serious lack of fervent prayer, God-focus and repentance *alongside* them. Indeed, the problem is treating evangelism as a mere "program" we can *do* without *being* in deep relational intimacy, surrender and empowerment in Christ.

To get an accurate sense of the present evangelism crisis and urgent need for a major increase of prayer, we must engage in an in-depth analysis. Points 9 and 10 help us take a sobering look at modern baptism and growth patterns. Unfortunately, it is often very tempting to look merely at surface numbers and miss the hard realities of actual conditions. Yet actual facts, ratios and numbers are stubborn things. If we look with thorough analysis, the plain facts often lead to very sobering truths about our real conditions and patterns. Evidently many denominations don't want to look too close at actual conditions.

Beyond question, today's facts and trends reveal a desperate need for major change of foundational patterns, *not* just a little tweaking of present trends. If all we manage to do is a little improvement of present patterns, we will surely experience severe decline (as the age-bomb and other factors begin to manifest). Clearly, we cannot simply continue with business as usual. We stand in desperate need of nothing less than an historic Great Awakening.

Because the next three signs are especially crucial, they received more space than any other points. Saints, it is utterly essential to fully assess the state of today's evangelism and prayer patterns. In many ways, these are the most vital and revealing of all the indicators. Since the facts are sobering, I again urge readers to remember, "God has answers for those willing to repent" We will examine biblical patterns for repentance in Appendices C and D. For now, please read the next three signs with careful prayerfulness.

9. *In spite of an exploding population, nation-wide baptism and church growth ratios have experienced unprecedented stagnation and decline.[44] At present, an astounding 70-80 percent of American churches are either plateaued or declining. Of the smaller percentage that are actually growing, significant numbers are by no means growing at rates equal to population expansion. Furthermore, we are losing far more churches than we are starting. To our shame, North America is the only continent in which the Church is not growing!*

By some estimates, as many as 30 percent of current churches will close their doors within ten to fifteen years.[45] As we have observed today's severe fifty year decline, it is most alarming this has occurred though the population has essentially doubled![46] You would think with double the population and greater numbers of churches, surely our baptisms would be up at least "some." At least for Southern Baptists, not only are our numbers *not* up, ratios are in fact *far* worse! (And this denomination is significantly better off than many.)

It is even more shocking that all this has transpired exactly concurrent with history's biggest explosion of evangelism programs, high level promotions, innovative growth methods, Christian education, ministerial training, organized prayer ministries and new worship styles. Our preachers and leaders are far more educated and trained as compared to fifty years earlier. We have *infinitely* more evangelism tools, marriage emphases, slick promotions and leadership materials. Yet during all this expansion of materials and promotion, the baptism decline and moral collapse has increased even far worse!

Today, unprecedented thousands of churches have utilized well organized strategies and quality evangelism tools. Countless millions have been spent in dollars and promotional focus. Yet the numeric decline and ratio collapse continue to worsen! Though good resources are certainly blessings, it should now be totally obvious they are *not* (by themselves) the primary answer. Otherwise with all the new tools and promotions, we would surely have seen at least some significant baptism increases. Instead, we have seen by far America's severest stagnation and longest decline! Saints, we cannot simply ignore these realities and continue the same patterns unchanged.

Of equal concern is the fact disturbing numbers of today's baptisms and evangelistic "decisions" so quickly fall away.[47] Though exact percentages are difficult to calculate, we certainly know the problem is very serious. In John 15, Jesus made it clear that genuinely empowered saints would *"bear much fruit that remains."* (John 15:5-16) The early Church and generations of revival certainly did just that. Indeed, they not only produced phenomenal numbers of converts, high percentages of their converts persevered even unto death.

Today's Patterns — John 15:5 in Tragic Reverse!
Much Fruit that Remains or Little That Disappears?

Sadly, many modern churches reflect the John 15 pattern in almost an exact reverse. Compared to the powerful patterns of New Testament and Great Awakening churches, modern statistics leave no doubt that most are bearing "little fruit" that quickly "falls away." Statistics leave no doubt we are often seeing far more shallow "decisions" than heart-changing, lasting "conversions." While early generations dramatically shook their pagan societies to Christ, we have essentially lost our own. In fact, we have gone from being a society that was at least somewhat "Christian" to one that is largely pagan and increasingly anti-Christ.

It is also significant to note today's collapse has occurred in spite of *far* higher percentages of college and seminary trained preachers than fifty years ago. While this in no way demeans or questions the value of college and seminary, it strongly reminds that training (by itself) does *not* bring New Testament fullness and power. For those who think education, programs and training are the primary answers, *please* stop and take an honest look at the last fifty years! Current realities provide a profound and humbling wake-up call as to the impotence of human training without God's full empowerment. One thing is certain — the devil is not the least concerned with all our cap and gown regalia if we lack fervent prayer, deep passion and true Holy Spirit empowerment. We must also never forget that God steadfastly resists even the slightest hint of pride or over-reliance on our own abilities, intelligence or strengths. (Judges 7:2; James 4:7)

Avoiding Academic, Theological and Denominational Arrogance
(Matthew 11:25 James 4:6: 1 Peter 5:5)

Today, we are further reminded merely having the right view of Scripture and theology cannot by themselves guarantee revival, vibrancy or New Testament power. (Though, of course these elements are essential!) We must sadly note even many of the denominations that have remained strong on Scripture have also seen serious stagnation. Though those denominations are *certainly* doing much better than their liberal counterparts, many conservatives have also experienced serious apathy and evangelistic weakness.

While maintaining high academic scholarship and biblical orthodoxy are *always* absolutely crucial, even these (by themselves) do not guarantee revival. Concerning fervent prayer and repentance, right "doctrine, scholarship and theology" *must* be combined with right "practice in fervent prayer, brokenness and relational intimacy with God." After all, the Pharisees believed every word of Scripture and were brilliantly learned (yet legalistic, proud, and powerless!)

Still another expression of pride is with some who may claim they are more "spiritual" because they have a particular view of the Holy Spirit. While it is certainly crucial to seek and experience the fullness and power of the Holy Spirit, bragging about it becomes dangerous. Besides that, many who claim to be so spiritual or "in revival" do not realize their baptism levels bear little resemblance to the generations that actually saw genuine revival. If we were truly spiritual by *God's* standards, there would surely be far greater societal impact and many times more baptisms. If some were as spiritual as they so boldly claimed, we would have long since seen a Great Awakening! Instead, the last forty years represent the worst spiritual collapse of American history. Friends, in light of today's horrific conditions, few (if any) have reason to be bragging about our great academic brilliance or spirituality. It is time to be humbling ourselves in deepest contrition, not exalting ourselves in bragging or smugness.

A Time for Honesty, Humility and Repentance
(Psalms 51:17; James 4:8-6)

Modern patterns demand that we *all* take a hard, honest look at low baptisms, congregational apathy and a conspicuous lack of true New Testament power. In general, the baptisms and social impact of even our "successful" churches fall tragically short of New Testament and Great Awakening churches. Given today's extremely low baptism ratios and collapse of families, the time for excessive bragging that "at least we are not like others" is long past.

Beyond all doubt, now is the time for heart-searching questions and examination. Indeed, if we are "so spiritual and advanced," why are baptisms and growth patterns so horrifically low compared to any generation of true revival? Why are dropouts so high and attendance ratios so poor? Indeed, why has our society essentially gone to "hell in a hand-basket?" If promoting (and sometimes boasting) about academic brilliance, doctrinal purity, evangelistic focus and personnel excellence were enough, why are we seeing so little that even remotely resembles New Testament power?

In light of today's extensive education, elaborate programs and highly promoted strategies (yet phenomenally low baptisms), it almost brings to mind the words of an age-old fable, "the emperor has no clothes." We might well wonder if God would not view "sackcloth and ashes" as far more desirable than self-congratulatory pomp and circumstance. Instead of boasting about our brilliance, fasting and weeping would likely seem much more appropriate. Dear saints, please understand these questions are not meant as arrogant or condemning. In fact, the questions are directed to myself as much or more than anyone. But one thing is certain — the time has come for honest assessment and broken humility before God. While deep humility is *huge* in God's economy, it can be so sadly lacking in our own. (Matthew 11:25; James 4:6; 1 Peter 5:5)

May God save us from a subtle pride that looks past today's true conditions and our own lack of passion, tears and New Testament anointing. We must resist the subtle arrogance of "making ourselves" the plumb line and measuring rod. Make no mistake — religious arrogance, complacency, self-reliance and pride are *always* among the biggest barriers to sweeping revival! While these attitudes are subtle and somewhat unconscious, they are nonetheless real and present on a disturbing scale. The very fact most have definitely *not* called themselves to truly urgent prayer, fasting and repentance is proof positive we are yet unbroken before God! In the midst of today's catastrophic decline of morals and baptism ratios, how could we not have called the most urgent solemn assemblies? By our conspicuous neglect, we are basically saying "let's just stay the course and try harder." Unfortunately, that's what we have done for fifty years. Do not the results speak for themselves?

Where Are the Tears and Solemn Assemblies?
(Nehemiah 1:4; Joel 2:12-18)

In light of today's desperate spiritual conditions, where are the Nehemiahs and Joels who call God's people to fast and weep before God? Indeed, the fact most denominational and seminary leaders have *not* called for thorough, sustained solemn assemblies speaks volumes. The fact most pastors have never led their churches to biblical solemn assemblies or deeply cleansing revivals speaks even louder. No doubt it is significant that our generation has been taught little or nothing of these utterly essential biblical practices. Many sincere leaders are simply not clear on "why" or "how" to lead saints in deeper prayer and repentance. (I include practical help for that need in Chapter Six.)

So what urgent message must we draw from today's appalling evangelism and societal facts? Simply this — to experience revival, we *must* bring serious, God-seeking prayer, contrition and deep repentance into the very heart of all we do. God is utterly holy and so must be His servants if we are to know full power. Prayer and thorough repentance cannot remain periphery side-elements to which we give only a little brief, passing lip-service. In past Great Awakenings, patterns of prayer and repentance were intense, central and sustained, *never* half-hearted, brief or temporary.

Today's evangelism and church growth patterns point to one urgent conclusion — we must desperately humble ourselves and seek God's face now! In times like these, God always calls His people to fast, mourn and weep for genuine repentance. (Joel 2:12-18; James 4:8-10) If we wept, prayed and repented as aggressively as we recreated, there would be sweeping revival. Instead of coming to denominational conventions for an eating and shopping binge, it is clearly time to gather for the most urgent fasting, weeping and prayer. In light of today's conditions, how could we do less? How could we even consider just rocking along with an attitude of "business as usual?"

Merely "saying" we need to pray and repent are by no means the same as "doing" it! Our generation has developed a disturbing pattern of thinking to declare an occasional theme or preach about something is the same thing as truly embracing it. In essence "talking without doing" is an unintentional (but real) form of self-deception and spiritual inoculation.

When Nehemiah saw the deplorable conditions of God's city, he *did* something. He wept, fasted and prayed for many days! (Nehemiah 1:4) One thing is certain — that kind of prayer gets answers! Dear leaders, where is the fasting and weeping today? Have we forgotten how to humble ourselves in brokenness, fasting and tears? Does anyone still seriously think we don't need to interrupt current patterns for major changes in prayer and repentance? Then what on earth are we waiting for — things to get worse? Just how much worse do they have to get? Beloved if not now, when? To God's praise, some key denominational leaders truly have a heart for increasing calls to repentance! May their tribe increase many fold.

10. *An honest analysis and full breakdown of most church (and denominational) baptisms reveals a shocking lack of impact in evangelizing the truly unchurched. Aside from membership transfers and biological baptisms, lasting adult outreach conversions are phenomenally low.*

Not only are today's baptisms appallingly low compared to the numbers of church members, phenomenally few of the baptisms actually come from unchurched adults. When we factor in the high percentages of baptisms that come from children of church members, rebaptisms of believers from other denominations and multiple baptisms of the same members, true "outreach baptisms" are shockingly low.[48]

Yet to get an even more accurate picture of real outreach impact, we would have to take the analysis at least one step beyond raw baptism numbers. If we were to consider the percentage of outreach baptisms that cannot be found just six months later, we would likely begin to see the full extent of the evangelistic weakness in so many churches. (Frankly, it seems some are not very keen on discovering that data.) Though I do not know of a full scientific study that has analyzed this on a broad scale, most pastors will quickly tell you the percentage is significant. In other words, of the already low number of outreach baptisms, disturbing percentages of these drop out within a very few months. With troubling numbers, it is just days or weeks. This leaves most churches and denominations with shockingly small numbers of lasting outreach conversions.

A Disturbing Contrast Between Past and Present Evangelism Patterns

It is significant that today's patterns stand in total contrast to the early believers and churches of Great Awakenings. Even with a terrible public image problem, the early Church reached astonishing numbers of adults who were complete pagans or adherents of false religions. Even their sworn enemies had to begrudgingly remark, *"These who have turned the world upside down have come here too!"* (Acts 17:6) Several Great Awakening generations came close to this same awesome impact as seen in the early Church. Compared to modern patterns, their greater numbers of converts not only remained in church, they shook their societies to Christ! Many even died for their faith.

In generations of Great Awakenings, rates of baptisms and growth were often three to four hundred percent greater than ours. (In some cities or regions, baptism ratios even approached a thousand percent greater!) Furthermore, far greater percentages of their converts stood the test of time. Clearly, something is seriously hindering God's full power in many modern efforts. To suggest otherwise, flies full in the face of Scripture, history and obvious current realities. Even today's more "successful" strategies seriously pale beside patterns of the New Testament and Great Awakenings. But why? Has God lost His power or is something missing in our patterns of experiencing His full closeness? Since Jesus is the "same yesterday, today and forever," I dare say we know the answer. (Hebrews 13:8) The problem is surely with *our* patterns, not God!

For the past sixty years, several denominations have aggressively promoted one campaign and program after another. We have gone quite far into quality biblical strategies like church planting and cell groups. And let me quickly say these efforts are biblical, well-intentioned and *certainly* need to be done even more! Furthermore, those who have faithfully labored are to be much commended for efforts to reach the lost. Untold millions have been spent in money, intense promotion and countless hours of sincerest, heart-felt labor. Yet when we objectively analyze "actual baptisms, true discipleship, net growth and real attendance results," we often get a most troubling reality check. For the greater part, actual results have been small and today's serious declines have continued mostly unabated.

There can also be a dangerous tendency to (unintentionally) exaggerate the significance of very small evangelism increases without an honest assessment of the big picture. Again, this certainly does not mean the efforts have been bad. It means we must embrace much more intense prayer, cleansing and fullness "alongside" all we do. Believers, we simply *must* come to a deeper experience of the relational "abiding factor" Jesus so clearly proclaim in John 15:4-8. *"If you don't abide in Me, you can do **nothing!"*** Only true spiritual abiding allows us to be fully God-focused and Spirit-empowered. We must come to understand that greater prayer and cleansing mean true closeness and yieldedness to Jesus. Greater closeness and yielding mean greater power with far more results and honor to God. It means the manifest presence and glory of God Himself!

Today, we must also realize that the few denominations that are a bit better than the average are typically nowhere near the patterns of Great Awakening or New Testament churches. Though they may claim to be "Spirit-filled" and "in revival," baptism ratios do not even begin to compare to the generations that truly saw revival. About the only way any current American denomination could claim to be "in biblical revival" is to be seriously ignorant (and somewhat arrogant) concerning the actual patterns, ratios and numbers of past awakenings. For this reason, many have unintentionally settled for *far* less than a genuine move of God. There is great truth in the words of the late revivalist, Manley Beasley. "We will have (spiritually) only that for which we are willing to settle." (From a sermon preached at Leawood Baptist Church, Memphis, Tennessee, Spring, 1976)

What's Gone Wrong with the Harvest?
Where's the "Power" and Fruit that "Remains?"
(Acts 1:8; John 15:5-16)

Today there is growing concern over the high numbers of "evangelistic decisions" that are never baptized and fail to exhibit any lasting change of lifestyle.[49] According to Scripture, such patterns simply do not reflect true conversions. (1 John

2:9) To assume (or casually assure) such people they are saved is both unbiblical and dangerous. We may well be affirming (and sealing) people in the deadly conditions of deception and false assurance. They now "think" they are saved simply because they rather thoughtlessly repeated a two-line prayer and someone "told" them they were saved. Tragically, their deceived state now makes them infinitely harder to reach.

We must also face the sobering reality that the "actual baptism results" of major regional efforts are all-too often small and short-lived. While mass efforts are vital and should *certainly* be done, modern patterns show nothing even approaching New Testament results. Again, this in *no way* questions the importance, validity and urgent need of conducting mass evangelism efforts. What it does reveal is the utter necessity of bringing deeper prayer, cleansing and full empowerment into every form of ministry.

Mark this well — without true New Testament fullness and power, we will never see New Testament results! That kind of power comes *only* from intense prayer, deep cleansing and genuine Great Awakening fullness. Unless our efforts are accompanied with strong levels of serious prayer and repentance, generations are doomed to continuing evangelistic weakness and decline. (No matter how many strategies we promote!) Furthermore, the prayer and repentance we practice must be preeminent and fervent, not some token half-hearted effort so we can say "we prayed." (Jeremiah 29:13; Joel 2:12; James 4:8-10)

Saints, we must quickly re-learn the undeniable truth that history's greatest evangelistic explosions come from deeply cleansed, prayer-filled believers and churches, *not* programs, promotions or events (by themselves.) In fact with most great moves of God, human programming was not at all central or preeminent. While we must certainly continue and increase strong celebration and promotion of all means for evangelism, it is equally (or more) imperative that we return to New Testament prayer and repentance.

Restoring An Essential Spiritual Foundation
Acts 1:8 "Power" Requires Acts 1:4 "Prayer"

When it comes to prayer, repentance and evangelism, it should never be *either/or* — it must always be *both/and!* There should never be any tension between "evangelism" and "prayer" people. In Scripture and revival history, true evangelism and prayer are inseparately united. Make no mistake, to pray without doing evangelism is false piety. Yet to evangelize without fervent prayer and repentance ignores an absolutely essential principle of spiritual power. It may also reflect a subtle (but dangerous) attitude of self-reliance. God forbid that we would think our programs are so good we can get by with only a modest prayer element and no emphasis whatsoever on deep spiritual cleansing of participants. And yet, since most clearly ignore this element, we evidently *do* think we can get along with shallow prayers and no cleansing or deep repentance. Little could be more erroneous or damaging to New Testament power.

One thing is certain — previous generations of revival didn't ascribe to these shallow views about prayer, cleansing and surrender to Jesus. And their power was definitely far greater! May we quickly return to the preeminent biblical truth they so clearly understood. "No one can know complete fullness of the Spirit without deep cleansing, genuine yielding and fervent prayer intimacy with God." While this kind of power is not complicated or hard, neither is it casual or shallow. The inevitable result of shallow prayer and cleansing is *minimal* power and *few* lasting results. In light of today's shockingly low evangelism and growth patterns, we must embrace nothing less than a full return to God's "missing relational foundations" of evangelistic power. It is time to humble ourselves and repent of any hints of self-sufficiency or arrogance.

In closing this point, I again stress that I am in *no way* picking on evangelism efforts or strategies! Beyond question, we would likely have been even far worse off without them. The Great Commission makes clear it is always right and paramount to share God's word and to witness to all people everywhere. The purpose of this point is to fully open believer's eyes about current conditions. Only the plain truth can move us to seek God in far greater brokenness, humility and prayer.

Yet please note, my most extensive analysis and concern is actually toward my own area of ministry — *today's prayer movement.* Indeed, if anyone's ox is being gored, it is more my own. With all my heart, I seek through this book (and others upcoming) to more faithfully foster God-seeking prayer in myself and others. By God's grace, it is my deepest commitment to ever move into far greater levels of personal prayer as well as equipping and encouraging others. Please carefully consider the next sign which suggests significant adjustments are still needed in today's prayer movement. But again, let us remember hope. By God's grace, we *can* experience deeper levels of prayer and repentance! As you read the eleventh sign of desperation, ask God if perhaps your own prayer patterns yet need to deepen. Appendices C and D are designed to move us toward revival-producing prayer.

11. *It is incredibly significant and alarming that America's baptism ratio decline and moral collapse has seriously escalated "despite" a much increased, twenty-five year emphasis on prayer, revival and spiritual awakening. While major prayer movements of the past produced huge explosions of genuine baptisms and church growth, most modern key indicators have badly declined.*

Though America's prayer movement is no doubt real and a welcome sign of hope, there are strong indicators it must yet deepen significantly. In reality, more books have been written on prayer, evangelism and revival in the last twenty-five years than the hundred years immediately prior! Today almost everyone seems to be writing a book on prayer and revival. Yet it is significant to note far fewer have been written on prayer's most crucial conditions — *thorough repentance, true brokenness and deeply cleansed, yielded hearts.*

It is further true that thousands of churches have started prayer ministries and prayer conferences are at historic highs.[50] For the past fifteen years, many conventions have adopted themes relating to revival, prayer and awakening. Many now even budget and staff for prayer and awakening efforts. Beyond question, all of the above are very positive signs and necessary biblical steps! Yet, in the midst of all the prayer activities, aggressive promotions, evangelism and book studies, a most shocking thing has occurred. Baptism ratios have continued their decline, morals their collapse and evil its unparalleled explosion!

In Church history, it is very unusual (if not unprecedented) to witness such a long, conspicuous focus on prayer and *not* see a major move of revival! While it is certainly not uncommon for historic prayer movements to take some years to build, it is *most unusua*l to see one go this long with so little measurable results! It is urgent that we seek to understand "why" this troubling scenario has occurred. I believe the following headings address some of the more crucial issues.

More Prayer "Fad" Than Heart Passion?
"Rending Hearts not Garments"
(Joel 2:12-13)

Honesty demands that we humbly acknowledge many of today's prayer ministries and prayer events are yet lacking in full New Testament depth, fervency and power. (Otherwise evangelism and church health would surely have seen at least some increases rather than today's severely low patterns.) Humility demands that we acknowledge much of America's prayer movement is considerably less intense or deep as those in Africa, Brazil, China, India and Korea. We also see much less Spirit-led fasting as mentioned so often in Acts and so prevalent in countries of dynamic awakenings. (Acts 10:30; 13:2-3; 14:23; 27:33) We must avoid the subtle temptation for prayer to become more a popular fad than true heart passion and brokenness.

By far the most humbling and heart-changing experience of my life has been personally praying and ministering with thousands of precious saints in several of these countries. Theirs is a level of fasting, fervency, passion and tears I have only rarely glimpsed in America. After personally witnessing the joyful passion and intense prayer of men facing martyrdom and torture, it is no wonder God's Spirit is so mightily moving in places like India. While in America there is increasing prayer "activity" and "revival talk," there is at present far more activity and talk than deep fervency, conviction or actual baptism results. Seeing what I have seen in other nations, God has driven me to ask searching questions of myself as leader of prayer and revival. Some of the following reflections may have relevance for others seeking to lead God's people.

Leaders — Do *We* Fast and Weep?
(Nehemiah 1:4-6; James 5:16)

As preachers and prayer leaders, we must reject the error of thinking merely preaching, writing or doing conferences about prayer is the same thing as being broken before God and fervently prayerful ourselves. There is a vast difference between being busy "about" prayer and being truly broken "in" prayer. Indeed, it is possible to practice prayer and preaching activities that are truly more "form" than heart passion. After all, we can indeed "say" the prayers and do the preaching voice inflections without genuine heart passion. That is unquestionably at least part of God's meaning in Joel 2:12 when He said, "Rend your *hearts*, not your garments" (as a religious performance or show.)

May God save us from the subtle risk of becoming prayer or preaching "professionals" who can skillfully say the words or deliver sermons but lack the personal tears of heart passion. God forbid that we would try and impress people with what we know intellectually though our hearts are not broken and poured out in weeping. While certainly no one has to be perfect to call others to prayer, we must have humble hearts ever seeking deeper brokenness and fervency ourselves. To God's praise, a small but growing remnant of pastors and leaders *are* gaining tears of passion for revival. And let us not despair weary servants. In our day of extreme busyness and attack, pastors and leaders can so easily become wounded (somewhat jaded) "professionals." Yet even for very wounded, weary leaders, God is restoring hearts of flesh for those of stone. (Ezekiel 36:26) God's grace can heal and revive even the coldest, most wounded hearts!

While there are certainly growing elements of hope in America's prayer movement, it is vital that we have the humility to acknowledge most of today's movement has yet to yield anything even close to sweeping revival. It is especially crucial to discover "why." Though it is possible the delay is simply a matter of God's timing, conditions are far too desperate to take the chance something is yet seriously missing in our fervency or focus. In my heart of hearts, I do not think it is just timing. I believe there are far deeper levels of brokenness, fervency and repentance we must yet embrace. This book is prayerfully dedicated to help us know how.

Motives, Fervency and Sacrifice are Everything!
Avoiding Prayers That "Offend" God
(Isaiah 1:12-15; Ezekiel 33:31-32; James 4:1-4)

It may well be that many are (unwittingly) still seeking God more to "avoid suffering and get blessed" than to glorify Christ and seek His kingdom and righteousness. (Matthew 6:33) *In fact, true revival praying is more than willing to pray for an economic collapse and persecution if that is required to bring true awakening.* Until we truly weep for the glory of God's Name and souls of men, revival will tarry. But let us take hope — God's grace can give us such hearts! If we desire and ask for such a heart, God will surely grant it. May we be satisfied with nothing less.

God indeed desires prayer that is fervent and confession that is thorough. It is sobering to realize God says shallow prayers and insincere repentance "deeply offend" Him. In Isaiah, He said such praying is like "trampling His courts." (Isaiah 1:12) God even proclaims that He "hates" and is "wearied" by shallow prayer and insincere sacrifices. (Isaiah 1:14-15) By such passages, we are reminded of the awesome holiness of the God to Whom we pray. Shallow insincere prayer emphases may actually "offend" Him! Indeed, little is more dangerous than doing solemn assemblies in a shallow, half-hearted fashion. Such prayer and repentance actually become a deep offense to God. (Amos 5:21-23)

Believers, we simply cannot risk several more years congratulating ourselves with today's levels of prayer, events and tools that are generally not bringing thorough conviction and spiritual awakening. In today's spiritual climate, we must also avoid any exaggeration concerning the current level and intensity of various prayer activities. Unfortunately, what is often called a "great" prayer conference or "special touch" of God today would hardly compare to the early Church, Great Awakenings or current movements in India and China. Just about the quickest way to kill revival is to start calling undue attention to our prayer efforts or exaggerating their depth and power. God never entrusts His full glory and presence to those with even a hint of bragging or exaltation of individuals or groups.

Religious "Forms" Without the Power?
(2 Timothy 3:5)

In light of today's horrific rapidly declining conditions, it is quite obvious that elaborate prayer activities, tools and promotions (alone) do not equate to true revival power. It is indeed possible and quite easy to have the religious forms without the power. (2 Timothy 3:5) Activity without brokenness, repentance and tears does not equal revival. While declaring themes and special events are certainly important, we must do far more. We must emphasize and teach *sustained,* top priority patterns of fervent personal prayer and deep repentance! Let us remember that united prayer efforts can be little stronger than the personal prayer depth and holiness of those who participate.

Indeed, if our prayers remain mostly shallow and issue from unyielded hearts, the results will almost surely remain minimal. (Psalms 24:3; James 5:16) Simply "praying together" or busily promoting strategies does not make up for shallowness and unyielded sin or self in those who pray. So does this mean we shouldn't pray together if we don't always weep? No, it certainly doesn't mean that because prayer movements often have to build until God grants believers greater fervency. Sometimes there will be months (or even years) during which prayer efforts gradually grow in depth and fervency. *All* sincere prayer is good (whether or not we always weep). We certainly shouldn't let the devil condemn or discourage our beginning prayer efforts while God is building our hearts toward greater passion. However, we must *not* be content to forever stay in casual levels of prayer and repentance.

While we cannot work up (or fake) true passion and tears, we can and must ask God to so grip our hearts. Indeed, sweeping revivals simply do not come from casual tearless petitions. Saints, we do not just need more people "saying prayers," we also need more people praying "effectively and fervently from deeply cleansed hearts!" (James 5:16) Make no mistake — only Spirit-guided cleansing brings New Testament fullness and passion. When our hearts are deeply cleansed and yielded, fullness, passion and tears will soon be present.

Be You Therefore Holy!
"For I The Lord God Am Holy"
(Leviticus 20:7)

Saints, we must never forget that above all else, God is infinitely holy. If deep, God-seeking repentance and evangelism do not become the major elements of a prayer movement, it simply cannot produce biblical revival![51] (2 Chronicles 7:14; Psalms 24:3-4; 66:18) Indeed, any so-called prayer life that doesn't focus around evangelism is false piety. Conversely any evangelistic zeal that marginalizes deeper prayer and repentance is dangerously self-reliant and seriously deficient of New Testament power. It is the kind of evangelism that gets "decision" but few lasting "conversions."

Concerning revival, all of Scripture and history declare the central preeminence of *deep conviction, Scripture-based examination* and *thorough repentance.* (Joel 2:12-13: 2 Corinthians 7:10) Today's challenge is that many seem to be promoting a weakened version of prayer that is somewhat shallow with little or no repentance. Undoubtedly, most of this is being done without intent or awareness. Indeed, few today are discipled or taught about fervent prayer and full yielding of heart. Many have forgotten (or never knew) that "humbling ourselves" and "turning from sin" must be deep, preeminent and specific, not casual, brief and surface. (2 Chronicles 7:14; Joel 2:12-20) In prayer we are to seek closeness with God Himself, not just His blessings and avoidance of problems. Indeed, surface self-focused prayer produces much "activity and promotion" but few New Testament results.

Returning to God-Focus and Deep Repentance
"The Key Missing Elements of Modern Prayer"

As to why there has been far more prayer studies, events and strategies than actual results, the following phrases reveal relevant light. *"The modern Western prayer movement has all too often been a mile wide but a half inch deep."* It has been much more about "bless me" than "cleanse, break and use me for Your glory. Typically, it has been far more "casual and brief" than "fervent, heart-rending and centered in repentance." Unfortunately, today's movement has too often been more talk, study and activities than actual prayer and repentance. Again, we must reject the notion merely throwing personnel, money or programs at a subject can (by itself) produce true brokenness and heart passion.

By contrast, the powerful prayer movements in China, Korea and India are often far deeper and much more intense. They also focus strongly on kingdom issues such as Acts 1:8 evangelism, missions, healed relationships and revival in the Church. They are also far less likely to draw attention to their prayers through flashy publicity or self-glorying promotion. It is surely no coincidence that these are the places God is sending sweeping spiritual awakening. Sadly, many indicators suggest America's personal and corporate prayer emphases are still too brief, general and self-focused to yield true revival power.[52]

As pastors and prayer leaders, we must ask whether we have (unwittingly) been guilty of *"healing the peoples' wound slightly"* or *"plastering with untempered mortar."* (Jeremiah

6:14; Ezekiel 13:1-16) These biblical phrases describe prophets who quickly glossed over and minimized the sins of God's people. They mostly shared positive messages of promised blessing when the far greater need was deeper cleansing and detailed repentance. Whatever repentance they did suggest was typically quite general and surface. As a result, their hearers did not embrace *thorough* repentance. False prophets generally cause people to avoid dealing seriously with their sin. (Jeremiah 23:22, 32; Lamentations 2:14)

Dear leaders, if we have briefly skimmed over (or somewhat marginalized) cleansing and repentance, we are drifting dangerously close to the same paths. Especially in today's sin-saturated churches, if we are promoting brief prayer without deep examination and repentance, our message is dangerously inadequate. If we are assuming (and proclaiming) that "God will hear prayer" though we gloss over repentance, we are trivializing His awesome holiness and misrepresenting grace. (Psalms. 66:18; Hebrews 10:26-31) Many in our generation have truly forgotten the incredible holiness of the God we serve. Amazingly, some actually speak of a "different kind" of revival that doesn't involve deep brokenness or repentance. Of course, the Bible knows nothing of such a "revival."

A "Different Kind" of Revival?
Great Commission Power Requires Great Submission!

A few leaders have even suggested the next great revival will be "different" and won't be much about cleansing or repentance. It is sometimes suggested that "if we'll just focus on evangelism and promote it harder, revival will take care of itself." While the sentiment is no doubt well-intentioned, the idea is seriously out of touch with Scripture and God's eternal principles throughout history. (Psalms 66:18; Acts 1:4; John 15:4-8) Biblically and historically, truly major revivals are virtually *always* about deep repentance, fervent prayer and Scripture-based conviction "alongside" intense evangelism. Beyond question, it is both/and, not either/or. In fact, if any generation *ever* needed even more intense examination and repentance, it is surely this one! Today's generation is unquestionably among the most compromised, fleshly and materialistic of all time. Without even realizing it, many are affected by subtle fleshliness, sin and materialism.

Only when hearts are deeply cleansed and filled can they know real evangelistic passion and power. After all, no one can "program" passion or "guilt" people into true spiritual power. While we must continually urge evangelism, only clean, repentant hearts can receive God's fullest passion and power to reach souls. We desperately need to understand the major difference in trying to motivate evangelism more from mere duty or guilt than Holy Spirit power, love and passion. Think about it — if aggressive promotion and strategies alone could motivate widespread evangelism and revival, would they not have long since done so? The fact they cannot should now be obvious to all. Indeed, with God it is all about heart and passion. *Only* prayerful spiritual intimacy and full surrender to Jesus can create that!

Seeking the "Reviver," Not Just Revival

Though the hour is deadly serious, let me again stress there *are* indications of hope in the Western prayer movement! Indeed, some elements of the current movement are simply too big to be of man's initiation. Furthermore, there are at least some signs it is now deepening its focus on genuine repentance and evangelism. And while the current movement has not been enough to offset today's dismal baptism and morality statistics, a few churches and associations *are* seeing growing results from their more powerful prayers!

While today's Western prayer movement has clearly not brought an awakening, God *is* moving a small growing remnant toward greater depth and fervency. However if there is to be any real hope of revival, serious prayer and repentance must quickly become much more a *top priority* and *sustained focus.* Indeed, the hour is unspeakably desperate! We don't merely need more prayer "activities," we need a whole new level of fervent prayer, fasting and repentance! Though of course we need more prayer leaders and preachers who promote God-focused prayer, we even more need leaders who also passionately pray, fast and weep themselves! Only then can their efforts to lead others have the fullest anointing and power.

Believers, we simply don't have another ten or twenty years for programs, prayers or "business as usual." *Now* is the time for much stronger prayer closets, prayer ministries and God-seeking prayer meetings. This is surely the time for all night church-wide prayer vigils and extended fasts. It's time to rend our hearts, not our garments! (Joel 2:12-14) In other words, it is time for deep brokenness and genuine repentance, not brief, casual pretenses of confession. It's time to seek the Reviver Himself, not just revival. *"Come beloved, let us seek the Lord while He may yet be found."* (Isaiah 55:6) In Chapter Six, I list several practical tools to help believers, churches and denominations do exactly that! Two tools are of special relevance. One is the book *Seeking the Reviver, Not Just Revival.* The other is a ten point *Prayer Covenant for Revival and Spiritual Awakening.* (See Appendix B)

12. *Several major Christian denominations have experienced devastating division over issues as foundational as simple morality and even the most basic belief in the authority of Scripture. Throughout all history, no group that seriously doubted Scripture has ever witnessed sweeping*

*revival. In fact, doubting Scripture virtually always
brings devastating spiritual decline and weakness.*

In several major denominations, doctrines related to even the
most obvious biblical teachings are now hotly debated (and
even often rejected) by alarming numbers. Many now have
trouble even seeing gross perversion as wrong. As a result,
denominations once powerful and evangelistic are now a mere
shadow of their former strength.[53] When they began to turn
from evangelism and Scriptural authority, they clearly lost most
(if not all) of the blessing and power of God. Their attendance
numbers have collapsed accordingly.[54]

The Deadly Fruit of Theological Liberalism

If anyone wants to understand the fruit of biblical and moral
liberalism, simply look at the history of denominations that
have embraced it. Take a long look at their baptisms and rates
of growth. How are they faring? The fact is, most are in serious
degrees of collapse and decline with baptisms almost
nonexistent! Extreme scriptural and moral liberalism have
always brought devastating decline and evangelistic
powerlessness to the churches and denominations it touches. If
any doubt this, even a basic study of church history will quickly
remove all doubt. No significant spiritual awakening has ever
come to a people who deny the authority of Scripture. That is
one spiritual principle that is an "immovable rock of truth."

Yet today it is deeply disturbing (and somewhat
bewildering) to see numbers of "Christian" groups who so
readily throw out foundational Scripture teachings and say, "we
have our *own way* of following Christ." One thing is certain —
none of us have the right to ignore Christ's essential doctrines
and legitimately call ourselves Christian. The Bible is utterly
clear that if we truly know Him, we honor and keep His
commandments. (John 14:15; 1 John 5:1-3) Based on a growing

number of churches that reject many of Christ's most essential doctrines, we are forced to the conclusion there are multitudes of well-meaning (but unconverted) church members. And of course, Jesus clearly stated this fact in Matthew 7:21-25. Tragically, a troubling number of "churches" have become mostly religious social clubs bearing little resemblance to the mission, practice or power of the early Church. (2 Timothy 3:5) Dear saints, churches either live by God's essential principles or do without His manifest presence and power.

Before closing this point, I need to share a word with any reader who may be of a more liberal persuasion. I in no way write the above statements with a mean-spirited arrogant attitude. In fact, my statements regarding scriptural legalism are made with great concern and compassion. It utterly breaks my heart to see what has happened to several once powerful evangelical denominations. There is no question their evangelistic vibrancy has been decimated by an abandonment of scriptural authority.

Furthermore, I have no doubt some dear souls are quite sincere in their liberal views and truly want to help people by "not being condemning" or "telling them their lifestyles are wrong." Yet God's word and overwhelming evidences are utterly clear. This path leads straight to serious decline and powerlessness! Saints, we never really help people by withholding truths essential to their ultimate well-being. (Even through telling them the truth may well cause some initial discomfort.) It is infinitely better to let God convict and save people by sharing truth than to affirm and comfort them on their way to hell. By so doing, we actually seal them in their deception and sin. Actually, nothing could be more cruel or unloving.

Please don't react defensively to this section. Instead, simply pause and sincerely reflect on the historical facts. Deeply consider the claims of Christ and know He will surely receive all who sincerely surrender to His Lordship. It is my fervent prayer that religious leaders and lay people alike would return to the true Christ and His holy Word. It is *not* too late, you can return to the living Christ! For all who claim the title "Christian," it is time to return to the Lord and Christ of Scripture. After al, it is *His* Church, not ours.

13. *Extremely high levels of church and denominational bickering, division and splits reveal shocking degrees of carnality in many modern saints. Not only is bickering rampant, many churches have functioned far more as inward-focused social clubs than red hot seekers after the souls of men. Virtually nothing more shames God's name or hinders evangelism than today's widespread church disunity and self-focused temporal priorities.*

At present, the Western Church is in a shocking escalation of internal fighting and disunity. Among the most serious signs of desperation is today's widespread rancor and disunity among so many believers. While Jesus said, "they will know Christians by their love and unity," many modern churches and denominations are far more known by their bickering, disunity and public battles. (John 13:34-35; 17:20-22) On disturbing levels, some of the more reckless Internet bloggers have now taken this global. Make no mistake — virtually *nothing* more profanes the name of God and hinders evangelism than angry bickering and disunity among God's saints. Especially when we have no more wisdom than to broadcast it to all the world!

It is even more disturbing that much of today's church and denominational division is actually more over policy, ego and personal interpretative preferences than truly major doctrinal differences. While fundamental doctrinal differences are appropriate grounds for parting ways, ego and policy usually are not. In fact, that kind of division has brought immeasurable shame to Christ and a profound grieving of His Spirit. It also reveals a most troubling level of carnality and pride.

Disunity — The Devil's Wicked Game
"The Church's Greatest Shame"

Historically, one of Satan's biggest tools is to get Bible-believing Christians to divide and argue over issues that are not truly essential. (Even though the argumentative always insist their issues *are* essential.) The spiritually immature just cannot seem to accept the fact truly godly people can disagree without having to divide or act as enemies. If some spent half as much time and passion winning souls and praying as pushing some lesser issue, baptisms would likely be double current levels! If believers truly understood our desperate situation and emergency need for repentance, many controversies would stop dead in their tracks! Nothing is more damaging (or foolish) than believers fighting among themselves over trivialities while deadly enemies scale the walls of our dwellings. Bickering, disunity and unforgiveness are among today's most devastating "devices of the enemy." (2 Corinthians 2:11)

The devil is indeed a master at getting godly people to elevate significant (but non-essential) issues beyond their actual level of necessity. The end result is that saints are divided, distracted and seriously hindered from prayerful repentance, evangelism, missions and sweeping awakening. Not only are multitudes distracted from kingdom essentials, the Holy Spirit is profoundly grieved and God's name profaned before a lost world. Contentiousness and unnecessary divisions are indeed some of the most devastating tactics of the enemy. These most damaging patterns are near epidemic in the modern Church!

Today's rampant division is no doubt saddest when it is unnecessary. In most historic moves of great spiritual progress, the devil resists God's activity like resisting the forward swing of a pendulum. He does everything he can to keep believers from taking right stands or experiencing revival. But once the enemy sees he cannot stop a positive direction, he often switches strategies. He typically then gets behind the pendulum and starts pushing people into actions and positions *beyond* what God intends! In past revivals, that meant some went into extreme emotionalism or other excesses. In cases of making needed doctrinal adjustments, it meant some kept pushing for even more divisive positions (beyond the truly essential.) In these instances, they took pet doctrinal or policy positions and drove them to a point of unnecessary division. Either way, God's Spirit is quenched and His people seriously divided!

One thing is clear — whether division is over essential or non-essential issues, unaddressed bitterness causes profound quenching of God's Spirit! (Matthew 5:23; 6:14-15; Ephesians 4:30-32; 1 Thessalonians 5:19) Tragically, the underlying division then greatly reduces God's presence and power in all we seek to do for Christ. Division and lack of love especially hinder our evangelism. (John 13:34-35; 17:21) These patterns also severely profane God's name before a lost world.

Ignoring Broken Relationships Means Ignoring God!
(1 John 4:7-20)

At present, a staggering number of churches and denominations are heavily affected by division and damaged relationships.[55] As vast numbers have fought and split, many tried to just "move on" without addressing underlying roots of anger and unforgiveness. Even when a parting of ways truly needs to occur, it cannot be done with ignored anger and bitterness. When we must disagree and even part ways, we must "agree to disagree agreeably" and release any anger. Otherwise, the Spirit of God is seriously grieved and quenched. Even when beliefs and stances are right, if our attitudes remain wrong, *we* are wrong. Arrogance and critical attitudes are among our biggest hindrances to God's manifest presence. We must immediately humble ourselves and repent of sinful relational attitudes past or present. Yet today, alarming numbers of churches and denominations have divided and split with little or no effort at resolving the remaining bitterness.

While countless others have not actually split, they co-exist in something of a strained spiritual "cold war." They essentially have a façade of unity yet plot and scheme behind each others' backs. Rather than the biblical command to talk and work *with* one another, vast numbers divide, politic and talk *about* one another. Instead of being forgiving, loving and positive toward each other, many are critical and negative toward other believers. Rather than obeying the clear foundational command to go to someone if you have a problem, many church and denominational workers talk to everyone but the person they are criticizing. Of course, this is nothing less than back-biting, gossip and slander. (Matthew 18:15; Galatians 5:13-15)

Loving God Means Loving Each Other
(Matthew 5:23-24; 6:14-15; 22:37-39)

At present, these patterns of bickering disunity and personal agendas are epidemic in many congregations, church staffs and denominational organizations. No doubt, disunity is especially damaging when it occurs between leaders and staff. Leaders, we must pray together and reconcile to walk with one another in unity. We simply do not have the option of staffs dividing up with each doing their own little thing. Such attitudes profoundly grieve God's Spirit in any church or denomination! It is very significant that the one place the Bible specifically mentions "grieving the Spirit," is in the context of angry, unloving attitudes among believers! (Ephesians 4:30)

According to Scripture, *no group* can move forward in full revival and powerful evangelism until believers are willing to humble themselves and deal seriously with damaged relationships and broken fellowship. (Matthew 5:23-24; 6:14-

15; Mark 11:25; Ephesians 4:30) Contrary to an erroneous modern theory, the "ends do not justify the means." When it comes to God's kingdom — it is so very much about relationships! Right doctrine or "focusing on evangelism" cannot excuse the ignoring of broken relationships. (Matthew 22:39; John 13:34-35; 17:21) Arrogance, insensitivity and pride can sometimes be uniquely subtle temptations for those with strengths in the all-important areas of doctrine and evangelism. For the most part, plain old pride and ego are now keeping millions from humility, reconciliation and revival.

Restoring Church-wide Emphases of Relational Cleansing
"Guarding the Corporate Bond of Peace"

It is utterly essential that churches and denominations get back to biblical processes for periodically embracing deep relational cleansing. For most churches, this process has been so long ignored, they are laboring under decades of built-up relational divisions and tensions. While there is no exact "program" for cleansing, there are essential principles for renewed love and fellowship. The primary pattern is embracing a period of relational examination and reconciliation by combining focused biblical sermons with times of corporate prayer. People are then helped to take specific guided steps to reconcile with others.

Another powerful process is having the church body (or denominational agency) pray through deeply cleansing, Scripture-based materials that are focused on relationships. As churches and groups bathe this process in prayer, it becomes a cleansing, reviving encounter with God, not an exercise in legalism. Churches can then conclude the process by conducting special services for experiencing renewed unity. It is similar to a solemn assembly but it is heavily focused on healing of relationships.

The resource, **Miraculous Church Unity and Kingdom Vision** is designed to provide materials and practical patterns for leading entire churches and denominational agencies into powerful relational oneness. We have had some phenomenal reports of God healing divided churches. (See Appendix D for this and other resources.) This practical step is something any church can easily do and yet the effects can change a church for years to come. Especially in today's Church, issues of healed relationships and unity simply cannot be ignored!

Though believers may "try" to move on without addressing bitterness and division, the Holy Spirit will not! (Ephesians 4:30) No doubt this is a central reason so many busy churches, denominations and strategies lack God's full empowerment. While believers doggedly hammer away with elaborate programs and promotions, the Holy Spirit is yet seriously grieved in their midst. Concerning relationships, the modern Church faces an utterly desperate need for humility, honesty and repentance. Seldom has such division, politicking and nit-picking so horribly profaned God's name and short-circuited evangelism. It is time for full honesty and humble repentance in broken relationships (past and present!)

14. *In disturbing numbers of churches, foundational ministries such as mid-week prayer meetings, evening worship, Sunday School, serious discipleship, expository Bible preaching and revivals majoring on repentance have either seriously declined or wholly disappeared.*

More and more churches are doing less and less in terms of serious Scripture study and multiple services of worship. For many, making significant time for church and sacrificial service has decreased significantly.[56] While many couch it in terms of giving people more "family time," the sad truth is services are really being eliminated because of rampant apathy and disinterest. Jesus and His service have become non-priorities for so many in today's Church. In reality, almost everything else comes ahead of Christ. Though we may try to give a "positive spin" to today's selfishness and lack of commitment, it can mean little else than rampant Laodicean-type lukewarmness. (Revelation 3:15-18)

Much of today's "so-called" emerging Church has increasingly embraced convenience, ease and self-focused shallowness over commitment, self-less service, church loyalty, biblical evangelism and depth of discipleship. Though wildly popular book studies have swept churches and denominations in unprecedented fashion, there have been no increase in most denominations' baptisms or general societal morals. While today's quality book studies have no doubt greatly blessed many, the overall result is nothing even remotely resembling a Great Spiritual Awakening.

Even after tens of millions have gone through various church-wide studies, for most denominations their already low baptisms did not go up a single point. In fact, disturbing patterns of immorality and falling baptisms have generally continued their precipitous decline. We must come to realize there is no magic book study or "shortcut" to true spiritual growth and biblical vitality. It is time to face our true condition and repent. We must rediscover and return to God's essential patterns of closeness with Himself. (Isaiah 58:12; Jeremiah 6:16)

15. *The last twenty years represent by far the biggest explosion of moral failures and public scandals among high profile Christian leaders and pastors. Modern history has seen nothing even approaching the vile scandals of the past thirty years. Such extreme patterns are in fact rare in all of Christian history!*

Never have there been so many highly publicized scandals and perversions among religious leaders. In America, nothing even close has ever occurred! Today's outrageous public scandals have brought immeasurable shame to the name and cause of Christ. There is now even evidence disturbing numbers of pastors and leaders are dabbling with (or addicted) to internet pornography. We have also witnessed a huge escalation of pastors burning out or falling victim to family breakup.[57] Accordingly, our generation evidences *far* less respect and honor for pastors, staff and church leaders. Pastors and staff being fired or leaving under pressure has risen to alarming levels.[58]

Not only are today's religious scandals and divisions more numerous, they are often far more heinous and widespread. What has occurred with the Catholic child abuse scandal is utterly unprecedented and horrific beyond words. Yet no Christian groups should become sanctimonious or overly condemning toward them. (1 Corinthians 10:13; Galatians 6:1-3) Virtually no denomination or corner of Christ's Church has been spared at least some serious scandal.

Also alarming is the rising number of leaders who have split churches by unwisely pushing new ideas and changes too fast and too far. Bickering, division, immorality and spiritual impotence have spread into nearly every Christian group. Readers need to understand what we are seeing is very unusual and escalating. Saints, it is time to weep for the shame we have brought to God's name! Yet if we bow in humble repentance, He will surely give us grace. (1 Peter 5:5)

In addition to gross immorality, we have witnessed reckless internet bloggers (from within congregations) turning personal grievances against pastors into a disgusting public battle for all the world to see. Little more profanes Christ's name and hinders evangelism. I tremble for anyone who would take ugly accusations and rancor in the Church and spread it globally. How many millions will be turned way from Christ by such actions?

This same pattern airs denominational battles into a public spectacle before a world we are supposed to reach. Instead, the public bickering makes us a laughing stock and fills national news stories. Whatever happened to the "common sense" of not using a globally public forum to argue deeply personal discussions and issues within the body of Christ? It is profoundly damaging when the blogs degenerate from discussing ideas to personal attacks and demeaning statements about fellow believers. How could we not see the tragic error of such an approach? It violates every scriptural principle of biblical fellowship, loving unity and concern for our Christian witness. (Proverbs 6:19; Matthew 5:23-24; 18:15-18; John 13:34-35; 17:21; 1 Corinthians 1:10; Ephesians 4:29-32) May God give us hearts broken over the abomination of shaming Christ's name before a world we are called to reach.

16. *In most denominations, alarmingly high numbers of pastors and leaders are nearing retirement age.[59] Catholics and many Protestant groups are facing a serious fast-rising crisis of biblically qualified clergy and lay leadership.*

In other words, the severe demographic "age" bomb is not only about to severely impact the "pew," but also the pulpit and denominational leadership.[60] As the population has increased significantly, overall seminary numbers in most denominations have not kept pace. This is especially true of those training specifically to be pastors. There is also enormous concern over the alarming number of seminary graduates who soon drop out of the ministry. At least for some schools, studies suggest as many as 80% of seminary graduates drop out of professional ministry within five years.[61] (Certainly these percentages vary and some schools indeed have better ratios.) *However*, the number is often disturbingly high even in institutions with the better patterns.

It is time to pray for "shepherds after God's own heart" and "laborers for the harvest." Far too many are essentially "hired hands" looking for the best position, easy-grow locations and highest salaries. (Jeremiah 3:15; Matthew 9:38) May God in His mercy raise up selfless sacrificial leaders wholly committed to the kingdom. We need men and women who have died to themselves and taken up the cross to follow Jesus. Only then can we be the vessels through whom God can send the next Great Awakening. But let us take hope and pray for shepherds after God' own heart. (Jeremiah 3:15)

17. *In terms of growth percentages, several cults, new age groups, atheists and false religions have seen unprecedented expansion while many evangelical denominations have witnessed unprecedented stagnation and decline.*

Is it not profoundly troubling when the growth patterns of many cults, false-religions, pornography and new-ageism far outstrip growth patterns of most churches? If it isn't, it certainly should be! Such patterns tragically profane and shame God's name before a watching world. Mark this well — when evil explodes and the righteous retreat in powerless defeat, God *has* definitely turned His face from empowering His people. Such patterns are among the most significant signs of the increasing judgment of God. (Joshua 7:7-11) There is no question a profound spiritual weakness is widespread.

For so many churches and believers, "the glory has definitely departed." The only proper response is deep brokenness, prayer and repentance! But like the lukewarm church in Revelation 3:15-17, many still believe we are "rich and in need of nothing" when in fact, we are "wretched, miserable, poor, blind and naked." There is only one answer — modern saints must fully acknowledge our true condition and repent in deepest contrition. (Joel 2:12-18) Whatever happened to the victorious, militant Church against who the gates of hell cannot prevail? (Matthew 16:18) It is time to weep for the shame our weakness has brought to God's Name.

18. *Of the relatively small minority of churches that are actually growing, troubling numbers are doing so at the expense of healthy balance, biblical holiness and depth of discipleship.*[62] *Some have adopted new approaches and philosophies with dangerous levels of Scriptural imbalance.*

Several have now become so "seeker friendly" they are seriously "God-offensive." They are often more like self-focused support groups than aggressive, evangelistic armies on mission to reach a lost world. Expository, God-centered preaching with solid theology and the "whole council of Scripture" have often been exchanged for man-centered, ear tickling sermonettes on a few popular topics. How different from the predominant pattern of the New Testament Church! (Acts 20:27) While America is literally going to hell, disturbing numbers are declaring mostly "feel good" popular messages on "blessing, success and temporal benefits." Far too many preach almost exclusively on what people "enjoy" or "want to hear" rather than what they really "need" to hear. Little could be a more classical biblical definition of false prophecy. (Isaiah 30:10; Jeremiah 6:14-15; Ezekiel 13:1-6) While we certainly need preaching on blessing and temporal success, the balanced whole council of God is utterly essential!

Without even being aware, many leaders have unintentionally drifted far into the subtle patterns of the false prophets in Scripture. In today's spiritual climate, it is very easy to be influenced by shallow, unbalanced models of preaching and ministry. Almost without exception, the biblical false prophets declared "blessings, peace and safety," when God's central message called for deep confession and repentance. It is very easy to be influenced by societal attitudes and ministry models that are popular but seriously unbalanced and unbiblical.

Based on biblical descriptions, false prophets likely had rather pleasant entertaining ways. (i.e. mostly words of "blessing, peace and safety.") Of course, this doesn't mean we need to be harsh speakers or uninteresting. Neither does it mean there is no appropriate humor or uniqueness in God's messengers. Yet true prophets generally function with a strong sense of spiritual gravity and holy reverence (not entertainers.) But regardless of their individual style of communication, true messengers will declare the "whole council of God" that deeply "convicts, instructs and reproves" to produce mature soul-winning disciples who disciple others. (2 Timothy 3:16)

Yet tragically, today's preaching is often far more focused on earthly interests and comforts than God's kingdom, righteousness and sacrificial service. Significant numbers have been seduced into proclaiming messages that are largely surface and incomplete. In some cases, the seduction comes through a wave of church growth books (some of which) are biblically unbalanced. It has also come from shallow congregations that want pleasant words instead of biblical balance with serious calls for holiness and depth. (Isaiah 30:10; Jeremiah 5:30-31)

Closely related is the tendency for churches to ask less and less spiritual commitment of members. It is significant to note this is the *exact opposite* of the approach taken by New Testament and Great Awakening churches! Yet for so many today, it is much more about convenience and self-focus than loving service and God-centered, obedient living. Churches pandering to this unbiblical attitude have produced decidedly negative effects on discipleship (or lack thereof). In terms of attendance, church loyalty, financial stewardship and Christian service, many members demonstrate dramatically lessened commitment, loyalty and depth (when compared to previous generations of older church members.)[63]

Whatever Happened to "Biblical" Standards?
Who's Church Is It Anyway?

Church discipline is another thing you will almost never hear mentioned in many modern churches. Yet, it is not only mentioned, it is *clearly commanded* in Scripture! (Matthew 18:15-18; 1 Corinthians 5: 1-13) How troubling it is to hear leaders say "discipline or biblical standards just won't work anymore." Are we saying we know more than God and that the Bible is irrelevant? While most would deny it, that is exactly what many are saying!

Indeed a huge need in today's Church is a return to "Bible-centered balance and practice." After all, who's Church is it anyway? Dear saints, it is *Christ's* Church! If it is Christ's Church, how could it not be based on biblical patterns and standards? Yet some modern leaders feel free to quickly re-shape and redefine churches by the latest good-sounding program, popular book or their own personal preferences. Unfortunately, some new approaches are simply not in keeping with solid biblical balance. For this reason we see churches focusing on one or two areas and neglecting other equally essential priorities.

For example, some will say, "We're mostly a "worship church" (but they seriously neglect discipleship and biblical repentance.) Others may say, "We're a teaching church," yet they badly neglect evangelism, prayer and missions. Others become "seeker friendly" to the point of neglecting any real focus on holiness. Mark this well — none of us are free to re-invent "church" any way we please! God's Word is clear that healthy New Testament churches maintain serious focus on *all* seven essential biblical priorities. (See Appendices C and D) While no church will be equally strong in all seven priorities, no biblical priority can be consistently ignored without severe negative consequence.

However, the above observations are *not* meant as criticism of all seeker friendly emphases, church growth books or younger generations. Churches can (and should) have a wide variety of expressions as long as they remain faithful to the essential God-given priorities of New Testament churches. Let me clearly state that contemporary-style churches can indeed have solid balance, God-given insights and impressive ministries. Unfortunately, several others are dangerously unbalanced. We must remember some of the devil's most effective (and deadly) deceptions are seemingly only a "little" off-center. Yet years down the road, the cumulative damage becomes catastrophic. When it comes to unbalanced church growth philosophies, a *"little leaven leavens the whole loaf."* (Galatians 5:9) Believers, it is time to define ministry, success and growth by God's standards, not ours.

19. *The overwhelming majority of today's "growing churches" require locations where population growth is rapidly exploding around them. Today's patterns are almost a tragic opposite of those of the early Church and churches of Great Awakenings. They grew by thousands of lasting adult conversions in the very worst of locations with extreme cultural, government and religious opposition.*

While there are certainly a few notable exceptions, most modern church "growth" is in fact transfers from other churches (not actual evangelism to the unchurched.)[64] In truth, the majority of today's growth is draining other churches of their members (though the growing churches are generally not doing this on purpose.) Much of the growth also comes by large numbers of people moving into the immediate areas of growing locales. If you took out transfer growth and baptisms of church members' children, many "growing" churches would barely be a shadow of their current size.

In order to see significant growth, most today need population boom areas, relaxed membership standards, high level entertainment, Fifth Avenue publicity and above all, massive transfers at the expense of other churches. In many cases their actual baptism ratios are no better (and sometimes even worse) than the tragically low averages in today's western Church. Yet they're usually held up as the models of success. It is essential that we stop measuring churches merely by surface numbers and start looking at their actual adults baptism patterns and true ratios. When we follow an accurate Biblical measure, there will likely be a significant re-shuffling of the churches we exalt as "successful." Friends, if we are located in booming "easy grow' areas, we should remember a huge dose of humility as to some of the major contributors to our success.

Sadly, most modern trends bear virtually no resemblance to New Testament and Great Awakening churches that reached all levels of hard-core unchurched societies in the absolute worst of conditions. (Acts 2:41-47) Though they had none of our programs, training, publicity machines, innovative methods or music, they did have fervent prayer, deep repentance and very demanding membership standards. (How different from so many of today's philosophies!) As a result, revival generations revolutionized cities and shook whole societies to their core. By contrast, we have overseen the worst moral and spiritual collapse in modern history. Is there not a lesson we urgently need to learn? Indeed there is! It is time to return to the "relational foundations" of fervent prayer, thorough cleansing and the prioritizing of biblical unity. *Only* these bring the type of closeness with Jesus that shakes the world. (Acts 1-2; John 15:4-8) Only these release the manifest presence of Holy God!

20. *Today's generation has produced an unprecedented explosion of new theories and innovative methods*

for growing churches. Unfortunately, several are biblically unbalanced and violate basic spiritual principles for New Testament, revived churches.

While some new methods are indeed powerful and reflect truly valuable insights, others are biblically unbalanced to the point of being seriously harmful.[65] We must always ask two questions of any approach to church growth and health. (1) Is it fully *biblical* and (2) Is it *balanced* to embrace all seven essential priorities of God-focused, New Testament Churches?" While we must ever seek fresh innovative ways for reaching people, there are specific biblical principles we can never violate and remain New Testament churches. Certain elements are "non-negotiable essentials" for true empowerment and spiritual vitality. Unfortunately, disturbing numbers of leaders are unclear about the New Testament church essentials. Saints, when we lack a thorough knowledge of Scripture, theology and revival history, we are easy victims for the latest fads and theories.

Yet tragically, many have bought into the belief that new approaches, methods and styles are the primary paths to renewal and awakening. In other words, they think we will see powerful evangelism, revival and awakening if they can just find the right approach or strategy and somehow push it harder. Both the Bible and history clearly show that notion is false. (The last fifty years especially prove the utter futility of promotions and strategies alone.) Such patterns miss the essential elements of God-focused repentance, fervent prayer and New Testament empowerment. They also miss the crucial element of getting God's unique vision for each church. Rather than being truly "God-focused," many churches end up just working programs. Unfortunately, today's unbalanced focus is not only false, it is exceedingly dangerous. In essence, this ideology becomes a subtle form of "idolatry" as we are placing our faith and central focus on something besides God Himself.

Biblically and historically, God is extremely adverse to believers trying to accomplish His work without deep humility and prayerful dependence upon Him. Only fervent prayer and deep cleansing produce biblical fullness and anointing of the Holy Spirit. Prayerless programs and philosophies amount to "chasing the wind" and today's statistics prove it beyond doubt! Rather than deep prayer and repentance, many have relied on human programs and strategies. God describes such an error as trying to "hew for themselves cisterns that cannot hold water." (Jeremiah 2:13)

Beyond question, our central problems are not a lack of strategies or innovative methods. *By far the greatest problem is a lack of heart passion, spiritual depth and supernatural power!* What we are missing is the "fullness and abiding factors" so clearly described by Jesus in John 15:4-8. While God-guided strategies are certainly vital and should be promoted, the main problem is certainly not a lack of activities, programs, promotions, slogans or methods.

While today we are witnessing a flood of "innovative new methods" for growth, we must always ask two crucial questions of any approach. (1) What "kind" of growth, and (2) Are these truly New Testament, Bible-preaching, evangelistic, missionary sending, prayer-filled churches? Far too many seem to think "if it is popular and draws a crowd, it must be right." Saints, we should well remember that Adolph Hitler, false religions and countless cults have drawn big crowds. Especially in today's self-seeking, materialistic society, merely being popular or drawing a crowd does not make a church New Testament.

Modern believers must re-embrace the primary commitment to build churches by *God's* standards, not the fleshly preferences of a pagan society. Sadly, the long-term fruit of unbalanced churches will not be seen for many years down the road. For many in the current generation, it will simply be too late. One thing is virtually certain — biblically unbalanced churches will never bring true revival and awakening to our land! Even though some may be popular, they are not God's means for truly transforming lost society. Regarding some of today's methods for "doing church," the title of John McArthur's book well captures a common dilemma of our day — **"All That Glitters Is Not Gold."**

Today we must face the reality that disturbing numbers of "growing churches," are doing so at the cost of biblical balance. As some boldly now say they reject the "institutional Church" for something "different," we must look very carefully (and biblically) at what they mean by different. With any new approach, we must always ask important questions like; How do you accomplish serious soul winning, deep discipleship and mission ministries? How do you keep Matthew 28:18-20 and Acts 1:8 as a central, predominant focus? What is your strategy for leading people into intense prayer and profound cleansing under Christ's Lordship? How do you help finance major social ministries, hospitals, train future pastors or organize major disaster relief efforts? How do you organize to address social issues? With the vast majority, the honest answer is — they don't!

Unfortunately, when we carefully analyze some "new approaches" to Church and Christianity, at least part of what we see is a selfish desire to throw off any real spiritual responsibility or commitment. They basically just want to do what "seems good for me and my own interests." It sounds much like a spoiled child for whom everything is "all about me and my convenience." Of course with such attitudes, serious discipleship and revival are impossible. And whatever is meant by "church" bears little or no resemblance to the New Testament.

The Bond of Peace is Not Expendable!
"Keep the unity of the Spirit in the bond of peace"
(Ephesians 4:3)

A related problem is the fact some growth theories advocate forcing fairly rapid changes on whole congregations without an adequate Spirit-directed process toward transition. The underlying idea is that the CEO-type pastor or ruling board basically decree changes and people can get with the program or go somewhere else. Some new methods even intimate that internal church wars are somewhat normal, necessary and expected. While some natural resistance is certainly to be expected, countless churches have been violently split and believers seriously damaged by forcing some new program too fast without adequate, God-directed timing and process. By so doing, the foundational biblical principles of "unity" and "loving the whole body" are essentially thrown out the window.

Saints, it would be infinitely better to make changes over three years (with relative unity) than to force them in six months and split churches with untold anger, hurt and damage. (Not to mention the public profaning of God's name through church bickering and fighting.) Because churches are to be a "family," we need to return to the understanding families are not corporations and family members are not expendable! To add insult to injury, it is often the senior adults (who built most of our churches) that get run over and tossed aside. For balance, let me add that most leaders who fall into this error do so unwittingly and with the best of intentions. They were essentially misled by some of today's unbalanced theories.

While churches definitely need innovative change, ever-evolving methods and new expressions, our generation is at unique risk of "throwing out the baby with the bath water." Change for the sake of change is very dangerous if not guided by the changeless essentials that constitute all New Testament churches. (Matthew 28:18-20; Acts 1:4-2:47) Unfortunately, disturbing numbers of leaders are no longer clear on the essentials of biblical churches. In a real sense, they are simply "winging it" while drawing heavily from humanistic secular principles and opinion polls. Many seem to be far more interested in the surveys of pagan thought than the essential principles of New Testament, Great Awakening churches. When we become too much like the world, we inevitable lose our ability to convict and truly transform. *"If salt loses is saltiness, it is worthless!"* (Luke 14:34)

It Is Not "All About Us!"
It's About God's Changeless Patterns

A related danger is with those who say they feel called to pastor yet think they don't need schooling or deep study of historic revivals. In other words, they think it is "all about us and our generation." Many think it is sufficient just to read a few popular new strategies. It is frankly arrogant for anyone to think they don't need to understand God's changeless ways throughout history. It is not only arrogant, it is incredibly unwise. (Hosea 4:6) Such attitudes leave us dangerously vulnerable to whatever new book or theory comes down the pike. The sad result is that we end up following "each other" rather than God!

Just because someone seems to have grown a church (or written a book) does not make their thinking fully balanced or biblical. Remember, several cults have grown big churches. And make no mistake — foundational doctrines and patterns and philosophies *do* matter! While God can certainly use people who aren't highly educated, we are all commanded to *"study to show yourselves approved unto God, a workman that does not have to be ashamed."* (2 Timothy 3:15) No one should make excuses for not studying consistently and thoroughly!

Since God's essential principles and ways *never* change, we had better make sure we fully understand (and practice) them.

As no other generation, we always seem to be looking for some "new method and magic formula." Yet many modern leaders have no deep understanding of God's "ancient ways and changeless principles" that have worked throughout all time. (Jeremiah 6:16; Isaiah 58:12) It is frankly ludicrous to suggest the relational foundations that shook the early Church and revival generations somehow "won't work today." The truth is, most have never really tried them because they are truly not clear on what they are.

Revival Generations Primarily Looked to "God Himself" *(Not the Latest Magic Theory or New Approach!)*

When past generations saw their churches and societies declining, they didn't place their main focus and faith in new methods and strategies to turn the tide. Neither did they look to surveys of pagan trends to tell them how to reach a society (though surveys certainly have value). Instead, they focused mainly on seeking God by His only path for true revival power — far deeper prayer and biblical repentance! Today it seems most are trying everything in the world *but* God's ordained paths of fervent prayer, abiding intimacy, deep repentance and true evangelistic power in Jesus.

Though methods can and must change, the foundational principles of fervent preeminent prayer, God's whole council and humble God-seeking repentance can never change! Yet today, most place far more focus on new strategies, methods and activities than intense prayer, Scripture and full repentance. The underlying theory sounds something like this: "If we can just get the right music, service times, dress codes or talk the world's talk, we can change society." Any real commitment to Christ's Lordship or biblical standards is typically tossed right out the window. After all, that might "offend" someone.

No Substitutes for Fervent Prayer and Deep Repentance!

Countless thousands do not realize sweeping revival and genuine power *never* come primarily from new strategies or methods. True revival power comes through intense prayer and repentance that releases the awesome presence of God Himself. To overwhelmingly major on shallow new approaches while minoring on deep repentance is the equivalent of "sowing the wind." (Hosea 8:7) Unfortunately, sooner or later we "reap the whirlwind." While some may for a time see a few better crowds, it is not a New Testament Church and it won't revolutionize society! Especially in today's society, mere numbers and popularity are *not* the primary measures. God's word defines a successful church!

Lest any misunderstand, let me again state that new music, innovative approaches and some seeker friendly ideas are helpful! We certainly ought to do everything we can (within biblical reason) to remove unnecessary barriers between Christians and unbelievers. Yet, while changing different styles and methods can certainly help, they are *never* the primary paths for sweeping revival, mass evangelism or social change. Unfortunately, many may not realize the error until whole generations are irreparably damaged by watered-down, unbalanced philosophies. Dear readers, we simply cannot afford to lose another generation! We cannot continue to produce shallow, un-discipled believers who lack power to win souls.

It is urgent that we not deceive ourselves into thinking different styles or temporarily better crowds are the measure of healthy churches and true evangelistic power. Sooner or later imbalance catches up with churches and denominations. If we sow spiritual shallowness, we certainly cannot expect to reap true depth and spiritual power. When we fail to create sold-out, soul-winning, disciples, we have betrayed God and those of the generation to come. Again I stress that many new ideas and approaches indeed have value and can be of help. However, with every theory we consider, we must always remember three great biblical principles. (1) *Is it thoroughly biblical and balanced with the seven essential priorities?* (2) *Does it follow the principles of strengthening love, unity and sensitivity to other believers?* (3) *Does it glorify Christ as the holy God described in Scripture?*

Leaders Please Don't be Defensive

To my brothers and sisters who may be using some of the newer church methods, please don't be defensive or think I am trying to put you down. For the most part, those trying the various new methods are wonderful people and have very sincere desires to reach people. Some of the methods indeed have good merit. Please don't think you have to totally change your uniqueness to embrace the seven church priorities. Indeed, there is *much* room for differing styles and methods while still embracing God's seven essential priorities. Simply evaluate the points described in this book and adjust your patterns (if needed) to incorporate God's essential principles into your own unique giftedness and community. Especially evaluate yourself by the seven New Testament priorities described in Chapters Five and Six. You will likely find you can still maintain your uniqueness while making real adjustments to more fully embrace God's central paths.

Saints, if we do not return to the foundational ways of genuine spiritual awakening and balanced church health, we will indeed go the way of Europe (which is total spiritual collapse). While new methods can certainly have value, we must never forget God's "ancient ways" that are our unalterable foundations. (Jeremiah 6:16) It is extremely urgent that we again measure church growth and health by the seven essential priorities of New Testament Churches. One thing is certain — with the frightening speed of today's moral collapse, we do not have the luxury of casually doing our own things or running religious experiments with the souls of men.

21. *Modern churches have been seriously weakened by a "skewed reference point" concerning evangelism, revival and church norms. In essence, modern saints almost entirely lost a truly biblical and historic "reference point" for spiritual success and supernatural power. We have begun to measure ourselves by ourselves rather than Scripture and revival history. Such patterns greatly damage a revival-producing spirit of faith and expectancy.*

In other words, what has come to be viewed as normal and successful today is vastly different from the distinct patterns of New Testament and Great Awakening churches. Because it has been 150 years since the last sweeping revival in America, it is easy to begin setting expectations and declaring success by today's appallingly low standards. Instead of true biblical and revival patterns, it is all-too easy to begin measuring by ourselves.

Over time, modern churches have become so accustomed to weakness and sub-normal experience, most no longer seriously seek (or expect) God's intervention in mighty fullness. Contributing to the problem is the fact detailed teaching of past Great Awakenings is rare in modern churches. Because so many have lost an accurate biblical and historic reference point, they no longer grasp what is possible. Sadly, even most seminaries treat the Great Spiritual Awakenings as something of an elective, periphery subject not required of pastors. While most leaders know God once sent Great Awakenings, they do not know in detail their awesome impact and what the same would look like in today's society. They even less know the exact patterns of prayer, preaching and repentance God used to bring such awesome movements.

Since few would disagree that a Great Awakening is absolutely our only hope, shouldn't every Christian leader be *required* to study them in great detail? The answer is obviously yes! Yet because such top priority focus is largely missing, few today are aware how much their personal perspectives, practices and expectations have devolved from generations that truly saw revival. Believers, we are unlikely to seriously seek something we don't even know is possible. The skewed reference point is extremely damaging for at least three reasons.

First, a skewed reference point significantly reduces believers' level of faith and expectancy. Biblically and historically, a generation's level of spiritual power closely follows its level of faith and expectancy. In Matthew 9:29 Jesus said, "It shall be unto you according to your faith." When believers start accepting depressed patterns as normal (or even successful), they cease to seriously pray for greater power. Thus if churches are not urgently *seeking* and *expecting* God's manifest presence, they generally don't see it. This pattern is especially dangerous because it is subtle and largely unconscious. In essence, we begin to "compare ourselves with ourselves" and thus lose an accurate, biblical reference point. Most do not even realize their perspectives are skewed.

When a generation's faith and expectation becomes diminished, believers then easily drift into over-relying on programs, methods, strategies and human efforts as substitutes for a manifest presence of God Himself. The prayer centered "God factor" is no longer a serious part of most expectation, planning or practice. Without even realizing it, congregations start trying to figure out how to "do church" *without* the New Testament power of God. Rather than seriously addressing *why* His manifest presence is absent, many drift toward manufacturing ways to try and function without Him.

A clear indication this is happening is when leaders give far more time and focus to strategies, methods and promotions than actual time in fervent prayer, deep repentance and substantial evangelism. There is little question this is the predominant pattern of traditional and non-traditional churches alike. In fact because they also have a skewed reference point, many contemporary churches are mistaking sensationalism, flashiness, popularity and easy numbers for a genuine move of God. Yet, in so many cases, actual patterns of evangelism, discipleship and holiness bear little resemblance to real evangelism, spiritual depth or New Testament impact.

Second, a skewed reference point is dangerous because it prevents believers from experiencing the deep brokenness, prayer and repentance so utterly necessary for true revival. When Christian leaders become content to major on activities and programs yet minor on prayer, churches seldom come to true urgency and repentance. Today's feverish activities and promotional hype can easily create an "illusion" of God's activity when in fact, actual lasting results are disturbingly small.

A subtle symptom is the tendency for some to declare "God is really moving" or we are "in revival" when biblically speaking, we're not even in the outskirts. A skewed reference point can cause believers to become proud and declare victory over a mere mercy drop of blessing. Such attitudes virtually guarantee we will never see a great revival flood. While we should certainly always praise God for mercy drops, we must diligently guard against pride and self-satisfaction with sub-par patterns.

Today there is a dangerous pattern of holding up certain churches as models of success when their actual patterns do not even begin to compare to the evangelism or power of New Testament churches. Neither do they compare with churches of the Great Awakenings. When we accurately analyze the actual baptism and discipleship ratios of most modern churches, few are biblical models to embrace. Remember, we never become truly broken and prayerful if our expectations are far below God's glorious desire and potential.

Third, a skewed reference point causes churches or denominations to become self-satisfied (or even somewhat proud) over results nowhere near New Testament or Great Awakening standards. Nothing hinders God's Spirit like the subtle pride of claiming to be more spiritual and empowered than results actually indicate. With a skewed perspective, churches or denominations may say "at least we're better than so and so." Again, when leaders become somewhat satisfied over relatively small results, churches and denominations have little chance of seeing true revival.

Assessing by Biblical and Revival Standards
"A Sobering Modern Comparison"

For an accurate perspective, I urge readers to calculate the following standards to their own church or denomination. Churches centrally involved in history's Great Awakenings typically had around a two to one ratio of attending members to baptisms. In other words for every two persons in attendance, there would be at least one baptism per year. For example, a church of 100 would generally baptize around fifty or more. Actually in the heart of some awakenings, the number was more like one to one or greater. In other words, a church of 100 might easily baptize 100 or more! These same awesome ratios prove true in larger churches as well. And while we don't have exact figures, we know from Scripture the early Church often had patterns even stronger than most Great Awakenings.

So how do we compare to the power patterns of earlier revival generations? For comparison, I will use my own denomination as an example. Among Southern Baptists today, the current ratio is no better than a shocking thirteen to one. In other words, for every twelve or thirteen in regular worship attendance, we baptize about one person annually. And again, many of these are small children and significant numbers of today's baptisms do not remain in church. I must also sadly note that many denominations are worse than these very low patterns for Southern Baptist. Unfortunately, several denominations are *far* worse.

So what does all this mean? It basically means our evangelism power and spiritual impact ratios are anywhere from 300 to 1,300 percent *less* than generations of great revival! It really doesn't take a genius to see something is catastrophically wrong. Beloved, we should be weeping in repentance rather than excusing, rationalizing or in any way trying to argue "things are really not too bad." But even as I make this point, let me also stress balance. None of this in any way means we shouldn't greatly praise God and celebrate every genuine evangelistic result great or small.

The above facts certainly do not mean we shouldn't highly promote outreach efforts and celebrate biblical efforts at evangelism. (Indeed, we should always sow gospel seeds as much and as far as possible). However, we must avoid the common imbalance of so exaggerating modest progress that we (in effect) gloss over real conditions and trends. Beyond question, it takes Great Awakening power and results to radically reach and rapidly change whole nations. Many generations before us definitely saw just such impact on their societies. Conversely, with current level of performance we are rapidly losing ours! While we certainly need to praise God and exalt what He is doing, we must never settle for less than *His* established patterns of success in Scripture and history.

It can indeed be misleading to declare victory or over-exaggerate progress when we periodically go up a percent or two. Even organizations in horrific decline are going to vary a little up or down from year to year. We should avoid giving ourselves effusive credit for small cyclical fluctuations that may well be incidental. Any real move of God would produce *profound* changes in numbers and ratios (not a few temporary percentage points). It is important to keep our eyes on the true overall picture. Indeed, it is vital that we be ruthlessly honest about our true condition. Otherwise we easily fall victim to skewed perspectives, false confidence or prideful boasting. Grace and revival come only to the broken, contrite and humble — never to the boastful, proud or self-righteous. (Psalms 51:17; 1 Peter 5:5)

God's Manifest Presence
We Must Settle for Nothing Less!

Not only did revival generations see enormous baptism numbers, strong percentages of their massive numbers of converts remained faithful and became dynamic, soul-winning disciples. Especially today, we need to remember Jesus' Great Commission command is not just getting "decisions or baptisms." It is making disciples and bearing fruit that remains! (Matthew 28:18-20; John 15:16)

Saints, if we measure our churches and denominations by the biblical standards of truly revived generations, it becomes quickly apparent very few modern churches can accurately declare themselves "in revival." A skewed reference point causes leaders and churches to become self-satisfied and declare victory prematurely. We then unconsciously drift toward being satisfied with activities and programs rather than the manifest presence of God Himself! After a while, we literally forget the difference. Nothing is sadder than God's people becoming so "accustomed" to living and ministering without His manifest presence, we forget what we have lost.

We've Never Had More Activities and Programs
"But Where is the Lord?"
(Jeremiah 2:8)

If leaders in any way gloss over real conditions or over-exalt the status quo, churches cannot grasp their true desperation for a greater move of God. In essence, believers get "accustomed" to living in sub-par power or serious declension. Sometimes as leaders, we quite unintentionally fall into patterns that contribute to this practice. Indeed, it is much easier (and safer) to nearly always be positive and affirming. Unfortunately, the moment a generation becomes comfortable with a backslidden condition, the spiritual decline rapidly worsens.

God can have little to do with people who are somewhat comfortable and self-congratulating in the midst of a great, growing darkness. (Judges 7:2; Psalms 51:17; 1 Peter 5:5) In the middle of all the activities and promotions, it is desperately urgent that leaders stop and ask, *"Where is the Lord?"* (Jeremiah 2:8) The Jeremiah passage describes the dangerous condition of leaders busily performing all their ministries yet becoming sadly oblivious to the fact God's glory and presence were mostly absent.

Yet when modern leaders and churches have a skewed reference point, they so easily drift into the pattern of the leaders in Jeremiah's day. While we are busily promoting a myriad of programs, we essentially become somewhat resigned to a spiritually weak condition. And though incredibly busy with ministry activities, few notice God's true glory is not in evidence! Decline is most advanced (and dangerous) when believers no longer even miss God's manifest presence.

Embracing Biblical Balance and Truth

As we consider these vital points, it is important to remember good balance and perspective. Once we acknowledge the fact our perspectives and expectations are indeed somewhat skewed, we should avoid two inappropriate reactions. *First*, we should not become discouraged, defeated or overwhelmed by our relative weakness. While we must be burdened to desperately seek God's face for revival, we should indeed rejoice and celebrate what He *is* doing. We should not fall into negativism or ingratitude just because we are not in full revival.

Second, we should avoid the passivity of getting spiritually lazy by blaming weak patterns on God's sovereignty. We should do absolutely everything we can in labor and prayer while leaving the ultimate results to God. It would be good to remember a key work in the title of Jonathan Edward's classic book on seeking revival. *"A Humble Attempt to **Promote** Explicit Agreement and Visible Union of All God's People in Extraordinary Prayer.......* While we cannot make the wind blow, we can and must do all we can to "put up our sails of prayer and labor."

After reading the previous twenty-one signs of desperation, I can imagine some may be wondering "what happened?" With all of today's education, programs and strategies, how did we come to such extreme decline and urgency? There is good news in the fact God's Word contains clear answers to those questions. The answers lie in recapturing the missing essentials by which God guides and empowers His people. The next chapter reveals the "biblical causes and solutions" to today's spiritual crisis.

What Happened — How Did We Get Here?
"If any lack wisdom, let him ask of God"
(James 1:5)

As we continue to examine today's appalling current and coming conditions, it is essential that we ask God "why" it happened. Indeed, we are not to be asleep but rather alert to God's sovereign ways. It would be the height of foolishness to just continue doing the same things that brought us to the current spiritual collapse. Yet, we will not fix anything until we truly understand why it is broken! Many times we think we know the problem when in truth, we really don't.

In the next chapter, we examine further signs of an imminent spiritual iceberg. However these final ten signs are unique in that they also reveal the primary "causes" of today's collapse. To a large degree, today's condition stems from certain unbiblical patterns that developed in churches and leaders. In other cases, the declines are caused by abandoning essential biblical patterns. In several ways, many modern churches and leaders lost key biblical essentials for relational closeness and power with God. Make no mistake — when churches and leaders drift from God's essential patterns, society drifts from God.

Get Ready for Change!
Ten Points of Empowered Repentance

As we will discover, certain relational patterns are God-ordained and absolutely essential for full New Testament empowerment. When leaders and churches move away from true spiritual intimacy, joy and power in Jesus, they lose the power of God's manifest presence. So much of today's drift has been unconscious and unintentional. Yet through God's grace, we *can* return to the essential paths of closeness with Himself.

I urge every reader to pause and pray before beginning Chapter Three. Only God can open our eyes to His truth and eternal ways. It is essential that we understand *why* we came to this point and *how* we can return to God. The next chapter fully addresses God's timeless requirements for New Testament power and radical transformation. Ask God for the wisdom and revelation only He can give. (James 1:5)

Chapter Three

Signs of Desperation in Church and Leadership Practices
(Signs 22-31)

I realize by now, some readers may feel somewhat overwhelmed by the pervasiveness and seriousness of current conditions. Little could be more obvious than the fact God's Spirit is seriously grieved and His judgment increased. Yet while we *should* be utterly broken and deeply burdened, we must *not* be discouraged or succumb to spiritual paralysis. It is time to "strengthen our hands, stand up like men and seek repentance." (1 Corinthians 16:13; Hebrews 12:11-13) Just as there are reasons we have come to the current state, there are God-ordained ways we can see a reversal! Praise God, there is still hope we *can* return to Christ in true New Testament power. As we examine the remaining signs of the imminent spiritual iceberg, I also outline the biblical solutions and specific points of repentance. Remember, God's solution works in any generation!

The signs covered under points 22-31 are unique in that they address unbiblical patterns in the Church that have largely "caused" today's overall condition. The following points come straight from the clear patterns of Scripture and history. These points reflect specific patterns that are utterly essential to explosive evangelism, sweeping revival and genuine spiritual awakening. History is clear there are eternal, non-negotiables we will either seriously promote (and practice) or do without much of God's power. Let every reader take hope! By God's grace, we can repent and there are helpful tools for recapturing the God-centered foundations of New Testament power. But first, we must thoroughly examine the signs and causes of the missing foundations. Please pause and ask God to give you a heart to hear His voice.

Signs and "Causes" of Today's Collapse
"How We Got Here and How We Must Repent"

22. *During the last sixty years, many churches (and denominations) embraced ministry models and patterns seriously inadequate for New Testament power, full Spirit-guidance and true revival. When we lost God's foundational biblical patterns for churches, we lost His full manifest presence. In essence, most settled for ministry models that marginalized (or neglected) intense prayer, deep repentance and biblical unity. These patterns are no doubt largely responsible for our current condition.*

In essence, modern churches focused on the five ministry functions (and other formulas) yet seriously marginalized the "relational foundations" of genuine spiritual power. (With minor variations, the five purposes are generally seen as fellowship, ministry, evangelism, discipleship and worship.) It isn't that what we have been doing is wrong, it simply leaves out some very crucial elements. Biblically and historically, the "relational foundations" of revival center around three elements: (1) *intense personal and corporate prayer*, (2) *deep personal and corporate repentance* and (3) *a serious focus on relational unity among believers*. These three elements are essential to churches being God-focused, Spirit-guided and fully empowered.

The relational foundations are the very essence of the "abiding factor" described in Acts 1:4-8 and John 15:4-7. Without these, the ministry purposes (or functions) simply cannot know full power. When modern churches marginalized or omitted the relational foundations, they lost the very essence of New Testament empowerment. While a focus on the five functions (or purposes) is certainly essential, neglecting the "relational foundations" is like forgetting the spark plugs and gasoline. Though you have an impressive car body and engine, the *power* is missing and it won't run!

There is little question the last three generations have focused much more on activities, programs, strategies and training than fervent prayer and deep repentance. *In essence, our generation has focused far more on the* **mechanics** *of what we "do" than the* **relationship** *of who we "are" through deep intimacy with Jesus and unity with one another.* Make no mistake — intense prayer, deep repentance and relational unity are *essential* to full discipleship and empowerment in Jesus! (Matthew 5:23-24; 21:13; John 13:34-35; 15:5-15; Acts 1:4; 2:1; 4:31-32) Furthermore, these must be "actual" top priorities of sustained focus and practice, not casual side items to which we give token lip-service.

It is very common for leaders to "say" prayer and repentance are top priorities when in fact, little actual time and focus are given to either. Though few leaders will actually say prayer is not a major priority, the level of practice tells quite another story. While this neglect is somewhat unintentional, it is nonetheless devastating to spiritual power. By neglecting a sustained, top priority focus on prayer, repentance and relational unity, we inadvertently doomed churches and programs to a severe lack of New Testament impact. It is also true that inadequate ministry models leave churches vulnerable to every new church growth fad. Countless churches have been split by leaders who grabbed some new (but unbalanced) approach and tried to quickly force it on the people.

If the last sixty years prove anything, they prove even the five ministry purposes, excellent strategies and strong promotion seriously lack power unless saturated and founded in fervent prayer, deep cleansing and biblical unity. Today, untold thousands of churches have gone through one program, book study, formula or innovative method after another. Yet baptism ratios and morals continue their precipitous collapse! In John

15:5, Jesus said it best. *"If anyone does not abide in me, he can do **nothing**."* In Matthew 5:23 and 16:14, it is also clear no one can be fully right with God if they remain willfully wrong with people. Absolutely, *nothing* can replace abiding in deep prayer, closeness and surrender to Jesus.

Until churches return to balanced biblical ministry and sound revival patterns, sweeping awakening and evangelism are virtually impossible. Today's Church is at a crucial crossroad! We will either mostly continue today's status quo or seriously return to the "relational foundations" of New Testament, revived churches. Are we prepared to make major foundational adjustments or mostly just continue with business as usual? The answer to that question will surely decide the future. (See Appendix D for steps of repentance and helpful resources.)

23. *Over the last six decades, busy believers (and many leaders) gravitated toward excessively brief personal devotions instead of substantial time in Scripture, prayer, fasting and cleansing. As a result, we lost the experience of true abiding and fullness in Christ.*

Make no mistake — when saints settle for shallow prayer and little spiritual cleansing, they lose the very essence of intimacy and power in Christ. Unfortunately, most surveys indicate shallower prayer patterns also characterize many Christian leaders. While it is hard to pin-point modern leaders' exact average time in prayer, there is little doubt it is nowhere near the prayer depth in history's great leaders (e.g. Jonathan Edwards, George Whitfield, John Wesley, Charles Finney, etc.) Because our busy society has an "instant mindset," many have adopted an excessively casual, "prayer on the run" attitude toward personal prayer and Scripture. Tragically, the "little dab will do you" philosophy has become the predominant prayer pattern of churches, leaders and laymen alike.

Busyness and Shallowness
"The Twin Destroyers of Spiritual Power"

Vast numbers have allowed the "busyness" of modern society to move them away from truly effective times in Scripture and prayer. We have so often allowed the "tyranny of time" to take a tragic toll on our spiritual intimacy and impact on society. As a result, New Testament-type intimacy and power in Christ are quite rare among busy modern saints. No doubt a contributing factor is the fact intense daily prayer has not been consistently emphasized or taught in many modern churches. Again, serious prayer is definitely not central in most church and leadership models.

Contributing to the debilitating problem of shallowness is an explosion of options for our time use. Today we are faced with vastly increased activities over earlier generations that saw revival. Even believers who would never watch questionable programming spend endless hours viewing sports or news programs. While of course, hobbies, information and recreation are important in balance, many saints are badly out of balance. Many devote countless hours to hobbies, sports, news or recreation and five minutes in a shallow devotional quiet time. Friends, do you see the problem? To consistently spend hours on hobbies, sports or various programs (yet pray five minutes) is a perfect prescription for shallowness and lost power. For many, the "good" has become the deadliest enemy of the "best."

For a number of reasons, disturbing numbers either have no regular quiet times or stop with one of today's short daily devotionals. While most devotional guides are good and can certainly be used, they were *never* meant to be all believers need! Think about it, if we always stop with the average brief devotional, where does thorough cleansing, powerful personal worship or fervent evangelistic intercession take place? The answer is — they don't!

Today's excessively brief devotions also severely limit believers' amount of Scripture reading. A scant few verses a day in no way reflect Jesus' injunction to *"live* by every word that comes from the mouth of God." (Matthew 4:4) Most saints have indeed stopped with levels of Bible reading that are wholly inadequate for true intimacy and power in Jesus. For this reason, countless believers are essentially biblically illiterate. Especially among younger generations, studies show staggering ignorance of the Word of God.

Brief Little Devotions Are *Not* Enough!
"They Were Never Intended As All We Need"

While quiet times certainly do *not* have to be excessively long, complicated or intimidating, they *do* require most if not all of the five basic elements of biblical prayer (i.e. praise, repentance/confession, intercession, supplication/petition and meditative listening to God in Scripture.) Especially the elements of cleansing, listening and evangelistic intercession need to be done with at least reasonable depth and effectiveness. (James 5:16) (Otherwise we're basically giving God a quick wish list and observing a mere token reading of His word.) By ignoring serious prayer and surrender to Jesus, this generation has been spiritually "watered down" regarding true depth and power. The promotion of shallow prayer patterns essentially "inoculated" many modern saints from experiencing true revival cleansing and genuine intimacy with Christ.

It is also true that few churches have prioritized the teaching of substantial kingdom-focused intercession or *biblical fasting*. But even the most casual reading of Acts reveals the preeminent practice of fervent prayer *and* fasting. (Acts 10:30; 13:2-3; 14:23; 27:33) Of course by fasting I do not mean legalism or requirement. (Neither do I mean bragging about it to impress others.) Furthermore, there are many types of fasts and individual leadings. Yet Scripture is clear that serious seekers will (at times) be led to fasting. When speaking about fasting, our Lord did not say *if* but *when* you fast. (Matthew 6:16-17)

By largely ignoring such issues as fasting and deeper prayer, millions of believers have missed joyful intimacy and power in Jesus. It is wonderful to be able to assure readers that powerful prayer and closeness with God are *not* intimidating or out of reach! (See Chapter Six for practical resources that provide significant help.) In light of today's moral and family collapse, nothing could be more urgent than restoring intimacy with Christ through deeper prayer and Spirit-led fasting. (See Appendix D for steps of repentance and helpful resources.)

24. *A troubling number of pastors and leaders have embraced personal ministry models that major much more on human leadership principles than intense prayer, spiritual empowerment and deep holiness before God. When leadership models are more humanistic than spiritual, true revival power is impossible.*

While some modern leadership books are excellent, others shift readers' emphasis away from some very essential biblical principles. This pattern is a major concern because great awakenings are founded solely on leaders with powerful prayer lives, deep holiness and balanced, biblical leadership philosophies. Unfortunately, far too many leaders now learn from books that focus more on CEO's, high-powered oratory and organizational strategists than highly empowered men of holiness and prayer.

While it is certainly important to learn from human leadership patterns, for Christian leaders the central focus must always be Scripture, fervent prayer, humility and Holy Spirit empowerment. Human leadership principles (alone) cannot produce supernatural joy and power. Only fervent daily prayer and deep cleansing can produce victorious power. No doubt, shallower prayer patterns are a huge reason so many pastors (and their families) are burning out and failing morally. Without truly effective prayer, we cannot know full biblical anointing and joyful passion. Spiritual shallowness is a key reason many churches and leaders see so little real New Testament power.

If Church leaders embrace inadequate prayer and leadership models, New Testament empowerment is forfeited and society continues its current spiritual collapse. In our day of endless programs and promotions, sincere well-meaning pastors can easily become ensnared in many of the more humanistic leadership strategies (and not even realize the error.) Today's unique danger is in the fact humanistic leadership philosophies are often mixed with Christian language and the error can be very subtle (but nonetheless damaging.)

Today's Widespread "Martha Syndrome"
(Luke 10:38-42)

Never have pastors been so busy or inundated with as many "good" ideas to try. But as we all know, the "good" can easily become the deadliest enemy of the "best." To use a biblical analogy, thousands of leaders are fully caught up in the "Martha syndrome." (Luke 10:38-42) In other words, they're so busy trying to work *for* God, they spend very little time *with* Him in deeper prayer, cleansing and spiritual fullness.

Pastors, we can easily become so busy trying new methods and leadership strategies, we inadvertently marginalize serious personal prayer, repentance and holiness. By so doing, we miss deepest intimacy with God and fullness of power. Scripture and history leave no doubt that intense prayer, deep repentance and total surrender are utterly essential to joy-filled intimacy and full power in Jesus. Close "abiding in Jesus" is the first and predominate daily requirement of empowered New Testament leaders. (Acts 1:4-8; John 15:4-8; James 5:16)

Today's pastors and leaders are under enormous pressure to embrace the "shallow on the run" prayer patterns of a busy society. They are also tempted to rely on human leadership techniques and strategies more than the full empowerment of God's Spirit. One thing is certain — when shallow prayer becomes a leader's pattern, he is very unlikely to lead his church or family beyond his own level of practice. Lack of fervent prayer and fasting in leaders produces the same patterns at church and home. It also makes leaders much more likely to merely work programs or act on human ideas than receive a unique, revealed vision from God.

While certain human-based strategies may at times encourage numeric growth in church numbers, they will never bring true biblical revival or Great Awakening evangelism (which is our society's only hope!) Only holy, prayer-filled leaders can receive God's unique revealed vision for their own ministry. From this alone comes true revival and power.

Fervent Prayer, Holiness and Spiritual Abiding
The "Essential" Principles of Biblical Leadership
(John 15:5; Acts 1:8)

Throughout Scripture and history, one pattern is central in the leaders who evidenced true revival and great spiritual power. That pattern was the powerful personal practice of fervent prayer and ever-deepening personal repentance. They also knew how to lead God's people in powerful *corporate* prayer and repentance. History's great revivals and evangelistic harvests *never* came through leaders or laymen with shallow (or even average) personal prayer lives! Revival also seldom came to churches whose pastors did not lead them into powerful, united prayer. Dear leaders, no matter how busy our society or elaborate our promotions and programs, we will *never* rise (in true power) above the level of our personal abiding prayer intimacy with Jesus. (John 15:4-8; James 5:16)

Indeed, the most preeminent and vital of all leadership principles is found in Jesus words from John 15:5. *"I am the vine, you are the branches. He who abides in Me, and I in him, bears **much** fruit; for without Me you can do **nothing**.* How simple yet profound! God says if we live in profound closeness and heart surrender to Jesus, we bear *much* fruit. If we don't, we can do *nothing* (no matter how many strategies or human leadership techniques we try.)

Based on Jesus' words, shouldn't fervent prayer, humble dependence and spiritual empowerment then be preeminent emphases in all church leadership strategies? While they certainly should be, so often these are either wholly ignored or marginalized by such shallow token emphases. Books and strategies can sometimes impact as much by what they "leave out" as what they include. It leaves the impression some truly essential things are actually somewhat marginal. As a result, many leaders model far more after CEO's, organizers and strategists than men of deep prayer and spiritual power.

Until modern leaders recapture the passion of powerful prayer and holiness, they simply cannot know full intimacy, joy or empowerment in Jesus. Without stronger personal prayer and holiness in leaders, the current spiritual collapse will almost surely continue (regardless of activities, programs or leadership training.) After all, the last twenty years has witnessed history's biggest explosion of resources on "leadership" and pastor materials. Yet during the very same period, baptism decline, pastoral burn-out, church splits and leaders in moral failures have continued their downward spiral.

Again let me stress I am *not* saying we shouldn't study a wide range of human leadership patterns and principles. I am saying based on Scripture and history, these should not be the continual predominate emphasis. However, we can learn to walk in proper balance and some of our leadership strategies are doing just that! Concerning leaders' practice of prayer and repentance, we are truly desperate for significant change, not a few minor adjustments. There is a central truth we must never forget. *"As go leaders, so goes the Church and nation!"* Yet through God's grace, today's leaders *can* return to revival-producing prayer and joyful intimacy with Jesus. (See Appendix D for steps of repentance and helpful resources.)

25. *Over the last century, an overwhelming majority of churches almost completely abandoned powerful, church-wide prayer meetings. Throughout Scripture and history, churches without powerful corporate prayer are churches without God's revival presence! Dynamic corporate prayer is a non-negotiable essential for truly revived, New Testament churches.*

Modern churches unquestionably embraced patterns that focused much more on new activities, organizations and strategies than powerful corporate prayer. Tragically, when churches abandoned dynamic corporate prayer, they forfeited an absolutely crucial element of New Testament power! Powerful corporate prayer is a non-negotiable, essential *requirement* for truly revived, Acts 1:8 churches! Along with Scripture, it is a necessary means of corporate intimacy with God and joint experience of His manifest presence. Yet instead of conducting regular church-wide prayer meetings, most churches replaced these with a Bible devotion and a brief closing prayer over a hospital list. Oddly enough, these meetings are often still called "the mid-week prayer meeting" (though they have little to do with kingdom prayer.)

Around the mid 1950's, churches also began to split mid-week congregations into many different groups doing just about everything but "praying" together. Unfortunately, such patterns bear little resemblance to the patterns of the early Church or churches of Great Awakenings. Even the few modern denominations that maintained some semblance of prayer meetings saw their main focus shift from lost souls, revival and repentance to concerns of health, wealth and personal blessing.

While we certainly need to have various groups and different activities, we must also make time for corporate church-wide prayer. (Matthew 21:13; Acts 2:1) Concerning good programs and prayer, it is not either/or, it is both/and! Biblically and historically, at least some form of kingdom-focused prayer meeting is crucial to revival and spiritual awakening. By "kingdom-focused," I mean prayer that is mostly centered on eternal issues like evangelism, missions, restoring broken relationships, revival, global harvest, spiritual warfare, etc.

For balance, I am *not* suggesting that corporate intercession is some magic program or formula all churches must do the same way. If done carelessly or as a rigid program, prayer meetings can be quite dead and ineffective. They also have limited power if we ignore the development of our members' personal prayer lives or gloss over spiritual cleansing. (Psalms 24:3; 66:18) Prayer meetings will seldom be much stronger than the prayer lives and spiritual purity of those who are in them. (Although good prayer meetings can also help strengthen members' personal prayer lives.) Yet when corporate prayer is practiced in a Spirit-guided fashion, the power is phenomenal! Prayer meetings then become a dynamic "living relationship" not just the latest program fad. There is good news in the fact *any* church can learn to experience powerful corporate prayer.

Church-wide Prayer *is* Our Corporate Intimacy With God!

Corporate prayer is an essential key to moving churches from merely talking and studying *about* God to actually talking and listening *to* Him. It is the very heart of our corporate relationship with God and each other. He must be weary of churches conducting services as if He is not even present! In most churches, little (or no) time is given to directly talking and listening to God. For many modern congregations, prayer is mostly a perfunctory ritual to begin and end meetings. Such patterns make very little opportunity for people to directly encounter and respond to God Himself.

Dynamic corporate prayer also includes patterns in addition to the weekly prayer meeting. In most modern churches, prayer time for kingdom-focused issues is very rare. Serious prayer in worship services is virtually non-existent. Yet adding even a little dynamic prayer can revolutionize worship services. Corporate prayer can (and often should) be more a part of many worship services and small group meetings. Biblically and historically, united prayer permeated the entire DNA of empowered churches. The abandonment of strong corporate prayer has profound and tragic implications for any generation. The conspicuous lack of corporate prayer is unquestionably an enormous factor in today's spiritual collapse! The modern neglect of prayer meetings has been devastating for at least four reasons.

Four Reasons Neglecting Corporate Prayer is So Devastating

(1) Neglecting united prayer violates Christ's primary declaration for empowered New Testament churches. Jesus clearly stated, *"My house shall be called a house of prayer."* (Matthew 21:13; Mark 11:17) There is no question Jesus was mostly referring to the "corporate" prayer of the temple.

(2) Shallow prayer patterns wholly ignore the central example from the book of Acts. As our primary guide, the early Church was both "born in" and continually "saturated with" intense, corporate prayer. Prayer meetings were no doubt crucial to their world-shaking evangelistic power and anointed preaching. (Acts 1:4-4:31) Corporate prayer is also a huge key to Christian unity.

(3) Throughout Church history, powerful corporate prayer is utterly *central* to virtually all great revivals and spiritual awakenings. History leaves no doubt as to the essential importance of corporate and small group prayer in revival, church vitality and sweeping evangelism. (2 Chronicles 7:14; Acts 4:31)

(4) Neglecting corporate prayer reflects a dangerous attitude of arrogance and self-reliance. United prayer is the essential way believers *unite* and *humble* themselves to seek God's mighty presence. Beyond question, God *requires* deep humility and total dependence. (Judges 7:2; 2 Chronicles 7:14; Joel 2:12-18; Acts 1:4-4:32) Though for most it was unintended, ignoring united prayer is a subtle (but real) form of arrogance and disobedience to God's primary ordained pattern for His Church. We are basically telling God we think we can function *without* humbling ourselves in fervent, united prayer.

In essence, when today's Church became too busy and programmed to humble itself in corporate prayer, it became too busy (and too proud) for God's mighty presence! Prayer sets the essential spiritual atmosphere in which God fully releases His manifest presence. It ushers believers into the essential attitude of true humility, expectant faith and total focus on God Himself. Yet tragically, most seminaries still do not teach the *how* and *why* of building praying churches (though some are now beginning to change.) There are also some early signs of a return to corporate prayer. Yet, this trend must quickly increase *many-fold!*

To fully address the urgent need for change, **Dynamic Church Prayer Meetings** will soon be available to all leaders and churches. It provides powerful inspiration and practical, instructive help. (In Appendix D, I provide a descriptive list of powerful resources from various authors.) Today there are indeed new tools to help any church embrace dynamic, revival producing corporate and small group prayer meetings. In my own pastoring experience, corporate prayer was unquestionably key to an explosion of baptisms and a lasting move of God's Spirit. The same will prove true for any church that chooses to unite in effective prayer!

The current generation desperately needs to realize activities, preaching, programs and methods can *never* replace the awesome power of Spirit-guided corporate prayer. In fact, united prayer is the central "power" for all else we do! Virtually no generation has seen sweeping revival without it and we surely won't prove an exception! At this point I must strongly stress the fact corporate prayer is not some optional opinion or personal preference. "It is a changeless biblical principle for empowered churches. Believers, we either encounter God by His changeless ordained principles or do without His full presence and power!" (Matthew 21:13; Acts 1:4; 2:1; 4:31) If you don't believe me, just look around at today's conditions. How well have we done without it? Beyond question, the current need to return to God through corporate prayer is desperate and non-negotiable. True revival and sweeping evangelistic harvest utterly depend upon it! (See Appendix D for steps of repentance and helpful resources.)

26. *Over the past century, the vast majority of churches abandoned periodic revivals that focused on deep, Bible-based cleansing and thorough church-wide repentance among saints. Churches without deep holiness and fear (reverence) of God are churches without full New Testament power. Periodic, Spirit-guided cleansing is a non-negotiable essential for truly revived, New Testament churches.*

By abandoning true revivals and corporate repentance, congregations lost yet another essential part of spiritual power and vitality. Throughout all of Scripture and history, periodic cleansing and repentance were "absolutely essential elements" of revival, awakening and evangelistic power! However, by periodic cleansing, I do not mean legalistic programs automatically done at set intervals. I mean Spirit-guided meetings through leaders genuinely guided by God. It is important to note the repentance that brought revivals always had three distinct characteristics.

(1) Revival type repentance is *God-centered, Spirit-initiated* and *covenant based.* (In other words, they focused on seeking God by His grace, not merely turning from sin.) Above all, true repentance is about knowing and pleasing God, not just "getting blessed" or "avoiding judgment." (2) Biblical repentance is always very *personalized* and *specific* with concrete steps of change. (3) It is extremely *thorough* and involves virtually *every area* of one's life. Of course, special focus is given to key areas of spiritual error.

Without exception, Old Testament revivals came from deep repentance as God-inspired leaders gathered the people to hear many Scriptures addressing the full range of their sins. Their response was a combination of deep prayer and thorough, Bible-based repentance. In the New Testament, we see the same pattern as Paul's letters directly targeted specific sins of the various churches. The message was so intense and specific he even "named" individuals and vividly described specific situations. Until God's conviction is both "strong and specific," true repentance seldom occurs. *"For godly sorrow produces repentance leading to salvation, not to be regretted; but the sorrow of the world produces death."*(2 Corinthians 7:10)

It is further true that our Lord's words and actions conveyed His intense desire for deep holiness in His Church. The instances of Ananias and Saphira, Lord's Supper abuse and strong warnings to the Revelation churches make clear our Lord's utter insistence on *thorough* congregation-wide repentance. (Acts 5:1-5; 1 Corinthians 11:28-32; Revelation 2:1-3:18) The same exact pattern of deep repentance is seen throughout all history. Great Awakenings sprang only from preachers who *thoroughly* addressed the specific sins of the people (though every revival had some uniqueness.) Strong evangelistic preaching was combined with deep examination of sin in believers. In historic awakenings, evangelism included an intense call to holiness and total surrender to Christ. Their gospel was not come to Jesus to get "happy and wealthy," it was come to be made "right with God" and "holy" in daily living. (No wonder their converts remained faithful at much higher levels.) After all, *God's* converts last — ours are the ones that don't.

One thing is certain — special times of prayer, deep cleansing and repentance have virtually *always* been crucial to sweeping revival and evangelistic harvest! These elements are also crucial to church health and vibrancy. Believers, if this principle is true (and it surely is), how could we possibly think times of deep confession and repentance are not still essential to today's churches? Do we think we are somehow smarter or better than earlier generations that saw God's mighty hand? If anything, we are far more compromised, lukewarm and worldly.

Yet in spite of the clear instruction of Scripture and history, a most tragic trend developed over the past century. *Congregations almost entirely abandoned periodic times of deep church-wide examination and repentance!* For so many churches, it has been decades since they experienced anything like a time of thorough spiritual examination and repentance. Most others have never experienced such an encounter with God! As a result, churches labor under years of built-up sin and unaddressed damaged relationships.

Modern leaders seem to think Sunday School and general discipleship can somehow replace the need for special times of deep church-wide repentance. Yet these approaches absolutely *cannot* because they are not structured for that purpose. While ongoing Sunday School and discipleship are certainly vital for spiritual growth, they are not at all arranged to examine and search someone's whole life in a fairly short period of time.

(Tragically, some churches no longer bother with even the most basic forms of discipleship.)

We are also a generation that has experienced an unprecedented explosion of popular radio and TV Bible teachers (and several of them are quite good.) Yet in spite of popular teachers and biblical studies on every hand, today's severe baptism decline, church shrinkage and moral collapse have continued their shocking downward spiral. While teachers and studies are great blessings and have definitely touched lives, the question is, "Can they replace the need for deep periodic examination and full repentance?" Scripture, history and current patterns clearly prove they cannot! Today's tragic pattern of neglecting corporate repentance developed for *eight primary reasons.*

Why Most Churches Abandoned Cleansing Revivals and Solemn Assemblies

(1) *As social activities, entertainment and materialism increased, churches (and leaders) became unwilling to embrace protracted revival emphases.* Modern "revival" meetings grew ever shorter and began to focus almost solely on the lost rather than the saints. Yet in many past awakenings, revivals were protracted because there was significant focus upon the sins of saints as well as converting the lost. In fact, the first focus was often designed to get believers right with God and one another. Actually, that pattern is extremely biblical and *essential* to New Testament power. Indeed, how can believers be highly empowered to reach the lost if rampant sin, materialism and relational division lie unaddressed in their own lives? Without deep cleansing, they cannot know full empowerment!

While evangelistic campaigns are certainly important and we often need more rather than less, they are totally different from revivals that thoroughly cleanse and renew believers. It is the deep cleansing revivals that have been almost wholly abandoned in our day. This sad omission has unquestionably robbed millions of intimacy with God, unity among believers and genuine power in evangelism. Alas, it has robbed us of the mighty manifest presence of God!

(2) *As churches became more apathetic, materialistic and relationally divided, strong preaching on holiness became less popular.* It also became riskier for Christian leaders. A major factor is the fact most churches are now filled with broken families and members who are at odds with other believers. Today's members are also more likely to disrespect others, attack pastors or sue their church. Thus over the past century, many pastors gradually succumbed to pressure to preach much more on safer, popular topics than the whole council of God. When this occurs, we are becoming "puppets of the people" far more than faithful messengers totally loyal to God.

(3) *High percentages of leaders no longer seem to understand that deep, periodic examination and repentance are utterly necessary for full New Testament power.* Because skills of leading church-wide repentance, revivals and solemn assemblies are not taught (or emphasized) at most seminaries, many leaders no longer understand their vital importance for revived congregations. Neither do they feel equipped to lead them. Throughout history, periodic Spirit-led cleansing has been utterly essential. Though certainly important, Sunday School and regular discipleship *cannot* take the place of periodic cleansing in which every area of believers' lives are laid before God in a fairly short time period (usually several hours or a few days)

(4) *Some have viewed calls for deep cleansing, examination and repentance as legalistic, over-orchestrated or human-initiated.* This false idea is sometimes expressed with the suggestion "if we just pray, we don't need deep examination. If we pray, God will do it automatically." There are serious biblical inconsistencies with each of these ideas. Of course, it is indeed possible that cleansing and repentance can be done in a

legalistic, programmed way (which will certainly lack God's blessing.) It is also true that more prayer does generally create a greater sense of God's presence and increased conviction. *However,* neither of these realities in any way means we have gotten past the need for Spirit-led cleansing, Bible-based examination, revivals and solemn assembly-type emphases.

One thing is certain — throughout both Testaments and all Great Awakenings, deep examination and cleansing were virtually always vital to God's empowerment and revival. Especially in today's spiritually compromised worldly society, how could we possibly think it would somehow be different for our generation? We obviously still need such cleansing because it is the clear pattern throughout all of Scripture and history! God unquestionably brings deepest cleansing and revival through full exposure to His holy Word. His central pattern is also to work through anointed pastors and leaders to call believers to cleansing and holiness. Saints, if we no longer needed emphases centered around His Word and deep cleansing, we could just ignore the biblical injunctions to search our hearts and repent. When it comes to biblical examination and prayer, it is not either/or, it is both/and! Biblically and historically, it is clear we must do both!

(5) *Some have presented the truth of our identity and union in Christ with an imbalance that suggests cleansing and spiritual examination are now somewhat unnecessary.* Unfortunately, this usually leads straight to spiritual laziness and passivity. While our identity and union in Christ *are* utterly foundational truths for victory, they do not mean believers can just claim their identity and "float along" with no need for ever-deepening repentance. Again, if that were the case we would have to ignore vast sections of Scripture. (Philippians 3:12-14; Hebrews 12:14) Though we are "accepted" in Christ and grow by "grace through faith," we must still walk in the Spirit-guided process of progressive cleansing and yielding. That comes mostly by exposure to God's Word for "searching and

cleansing our hearts." (Psalms 139:23-24; Lamentations 3:40; 2 Corinthians 7:1)

(6) *Many modern saints have embraced a "bless me-coast-along" mentality and ignore Paul's commands to "press toward the mark and perfect holiness in the fear of God."* (2 Corinthians 7:1; Philippians 3:14) By so doing, these saints forever remain immature and shallow. God calls no Christian to merely float along and get blessed. We are to "examine ourselves" and "pursue holiness" in His grace. (1 Corinthians 11:28; Hebrews 12:14) Deep periodic cleansing and repentance are absolutely crucial to that process!

(7) *Many truly sense no urgent need for deep periodic cleansing and repentance.* We have now functioned for so long on a sub-par level, most may not realize how sub-par we really are. Others will actually say they don't think we need such emphases because we have Sunday School. In light of today's catastrophic spiritual collapse and weakness, how could we possibly think we don't need times of deep examination? And yet if we are not practicing periodic repentance, we either think we don't need to, don't care or we don't know how. God's grace can help us immediately turn from the utter fallacy of these positions. For the many sincere people who truly don't know how to embrace deep cleansing and repentance, God has clear answers (which I will highlight later.)

(8) *Many ministers have preached predominately on things other than deep holiness, total surrender and aggressive soul-winning for Christ.* In many cases, it has been the subtle problem of the "good" becoming the deadliest enemy of the "best." In other words, many have preached so much on "favorite" or "popular" topics that deep examination and total surrender to Christ are seldom (or never) the main focus. Indeed, some preach so much about prophecy, family, miracles, financial success or blessings, they seriously ignore deep repentance and full surrender. For the most part, leaders and churches that fall into this error are well-meaning, good people.

They honestly don't realize their central focus has slowly drifted from God's central focus for this urgent moment in history. Yet as a result, their congregations can never see genuine revival. While they may have good crowds that "enjoy the sermons," they do not see explosive numbers of salvations, deep repentance or sweeping revival.

We *Can* Recapture Grace-Based Repentance!

For several reasons, today's Church faces a desperate need to return to God through deep biblical examination, fervent prayer and thorough repentance. In light of today's moral collapse, it is frankly hard to imagine how any leader would not realize the desperate need for deep Spirit-guided cleansing. In fact, if any generation *ever* needed such repentance, it is surely ours! Any idea we can be fully empowered without deep repentance is completely unscriptural. Such attitudes and beliefs represent a serious misunderstanding of God's holiness and requirement of full spiritual empowerment. All the programs on earth cannot substitute for fervent prayer, deep periodic repentance and full surrender to Christ's lordship! Only by this path can we walk in full loving fellowship with our God.

The idea modern churches are somehow "past the need for deep personal examination and repentance" is frankly ludicrous. Any suggestion "it just won't work today" is a serious cop-out. There is no question that God has always used deep church-wide cleansing to move His people into real repentance. While the forms and formats of the process certainly vary, the principle does not. Saints, we must keep our eyes open for error and imbalance in modern emphases. If modern theories start sounding different from God's Word and His distinct pattern in history, major red flags should rise immediately. Since God and His basic principles don't change, guess who is off track? (Malachi 3:6; James 1:17) It certainly isn't God or His Word!

Believers, it is time to return to God by His central ordained path of Bible-centered examination, prayerful repentance and renewal. No person, church or denomination can function in full power without periodic, Spirit-led cleansing and repentance. (See Chapter Six for dynamic practical resources for conducting God-led church-wide cleansing, renewal and dynamic solemn assemblies.) Though the need is urgent, let all churches take hope. By God's grace, we *can* return to deep Spirit-led cleansing and renewal! (See Appendix D for steps of repentance and helpful resources.)

27. *There is strong indication the American Church contains an alarming number of unconverted members. Evidence further suggests many who are indeed likely saved, do not have "full assurance" of salvation and thus lack overcoming power and victory.*[66]

Today's strong evidence of lost church members primarily consists of four elements. (1) Large numbers of church members give erroneous answers to doctrinal surveys, (2) widespread immoral lifestyles among members, (3) extremely poor church attendance ratios and (4) vast numbers evidence more of a nominal ritualistic religion than a personal relationship with Christ. Of course, each one of these patterns is biblically inconsistent with genuine salvation.

There is further indication some modern evangelism techniques have contributed to a massive flood of false converts. Based on the clear teachings of Scripture, certain patterns are inconsistent with truly born-again Christians. God's word is clear that the marks of genuine salvation include the "fruit" of a changed life and a desire to follow Christ in holy living. (Matthew 7:16; 1 John 2:4) When peoples' life patterns are seriously inconsistent with Scripture, we must assume they are likely lost regardless of a past religious profession or church membership. While we are no one's judge, such patterns call for gravest concern for eternal souls.

Current records and surveys leave no doubt that alarming numbers of church members virtually never attend, have outwardly immoral lifestyles and give totally wrong answers to surveys of basic salvation doctrine. According to Scripture, it is virtually impossible that truly saved persons would consistently exhibit any one of these conditions. Yet today, disturbing numbers of church members exhibit all three!

In previous generations, many Great Awakenings actually started with lost church members finding Christ. Based on strong evidence, our generation stands in urgent need of just such a movement. I am convinced the first stage in a modern revival will likely be large numbers of conversions among church members. Many believers must also come into full assurance. To address their need, we offer a key resource entitled, **Saved, Certain and Transformed: *"Journey to Biblical Salvation, Full Assurance and Personal Revival."*** This book is a biblical tool to reach unconverted church members, deliver believers from doubt and guide all saints into dynamic prayer and victorious living. It is carefully done in a manner that is balanced and thorough yet in no way operates as a "scare tactic" to create doubt. The tool is for individuals, small groups and whole congregations. (See Appendix D)

Dangerously Shallow Gospel Presentations

Contributing to today's problem is a trend among some to utilize dangerously shallow, incomplete approaches in evangelism. Over the last sixty years, patterns such as the "prosperity gospel" became all-too common. Another dangerous pattern is the "love, joy and peace gospel." In this and other shallow approaches, listeners are given an incomplete (excessively brief) presentation that focuses almost entirely on coming to Jesus for "happiness, success or peace." Little or nothing is said about God's holiness and true repentance is either quickly glossed over or ignored entirely.

God is presented as little more than a glorified "Santa Claus" figure. While some are actually saved (in spite of) such an incomplete message, countless others make shallow decisions that fail to convert the soul. Worse yet, they now believe they are saved simply because they casually mouthed some prayer (they didn't mean), joined a church or someone "told" them they were saved. Make no mistake — shallow approaches were *never* the pattern in the New Testament or the churches of Great Awakenings. Such approaches bear little resemblance to the preaching of Jesus, the early Church and the powerful preachers of history's mighty revivals. (Wonder who has it right?)

A related danger is vast numbers of churches that simply do not preach the utter necessity of "new birth" and conversion. In these churches, messages are mostly about social lessons or temporal struggles. Strong messages on eternal judgment and salvation are essentially ignored. It is also true that many churches receive members in ways that place little or no emphasis on insuring that inquirers are genuinely saved. Both of these common patterns are a perfect prescription for producing millions of lost church members.

Today we can trace a variety of factors contributing to large numbers of unconverted church members. In many ways, lost church members are an inevitable result of all the factors discussed in many of the previous points. Even more tragic is the fact most dear souls are unconscious victims of church patterns that are unbiblical. If a generation abandons deep personal prayer, neglects prayer meetings, avoids church-wide repentance and utilizes shallow evangelism or preaching, how could there *not* be legions of people who are religious but lost? All of the aforementioned conditions have led us to a point of supreme danger. That danger comes from two primary sources. (a) The natural sowing and reaping consequences of blatant sin and (b) the righteous judgment of a holy God. (Galatians 6:9; Hebrews 10:26-31) See Appendix D for steps of repentance and helpful resources.

28. *Over the past century, much preaching moved away from proclaiming sound Scriptural theology, biblical grace, a high view of God, hallowing His name, sin's accountability and strong expository preaching of God's "whole council." In essence, many have unwittingly sought to create a "god" in their own image. The subtle attitude is to have God serve us rather than us serve Him.*

Unfortunately, many churches moved far away from emphasizing the pre-eminence and reverential fear of Holy God. Closely related is a faulty view of grace that is shallow and devoid of human accountability to walk in holiness. This problem is seen in believers on both sides of the election /sovereignty question. Instead of presenting a balanced view of God as both holy and loving, many today began to depict Him more as a "buddy" or "success and wealth coach." The result is a serious loss of the reverential fear of God, tolerance of sin and a cheap view of grace. While God certainly is our greatest friend, He is not a casual "pal" we bend to our own wishes. When a Church and nation loses the biblical fear of God, sin abounds and spiritual power collapses. Beyond question, such is the condition of alarming numbers of American churches.

In a sense, many began to more or less "deify man" and "humanize God." This pattern is reflected in preaching or church emphases that focus far more on human comforts and earthly success than holiness, surrender and sacrificial service to God. When sermons tend to focus on a few popular subjects instead of God's whole council, some are essentially trying to create a "god in their own image." Many seem to want a "god" they can control and use for their own purposes. While most drift into these patterns unconsciously, they are nonetheless profoundly real and damaging. Many in today's Church desperately need to return to God as proclaimed in Scripture.

Proclaiming God's Full Nature and Holiness

It is indeed crucial that modern churches return to proclaiming the full nature of God. Saints, if our theology is incomplete or wrong, everything else will be wrong. Make no mistake — all knowledge and wisdom begins with the knowledge of God! When we truly see God as He is, we see ourselves, life and eternity as it is. It is time that we give believers the whole council of God's nature rather than a shallow version of our own making.

A related pattern of deep concern is the fact so many preach on a few popular topics instead of expository messages from God's whole word. Strong biblical preaching and balanced theology are truly essential to historic awakenings and revivals. Throughout all history, no great revival has come to believers with a shallow, unbalanced view of God and high tolerance for sin. Today's Church must return to the biblical God and a balanced understanding of our "accountability under grace." Without these foundational elements of Scripture and theology, true revival is virtually impossible!

29. *Many American churches became so micro-managed and rigid in their worship and prayer scheduling, they essentially "programmed" God right out of the mix. While revival "requires" serious opportunities for deep encounter, the vast majority of churches have no open-ended services or prayer meetings where people are encouraged (and led) to truly respond to God.*

Historically, there has *never* been a mighty move of God when the Holy Spirit was strictly dictated by a clock! While this certainly doesn't mean all services should be long or schedules ignored, it does mean churches must embrace greater sensitivity and responsiveness to God's Spirit. We must at least give ourselves the "opportunity" to respond to God in fervent prayer and repentance. Obviously, some services may need to mostly adhere to a schedule for reasons of logistics and coordination of multiple groups of people. Yet some services should indeed be scheduled longer or at least planned so people can have time to respond in meaningful prayer and surrender. Indeed, there is much power in making some services "open-ended" in that people can either continue in prayer or quietly leave.

In history's Great Awakenings, leaders fully understood the importance of having at least some services with significant opportunity for people to respond to God and each other. Unfortunately in many American churches, there is not a single service or small group structured so people can freely respond in prayer, sharing and repentance. For most churches, meetings and groups, everything is so regimented, controlled (and dead) God would have to force His way to any real manifestation. *In other words, God's manifest presence is not anticipated, planned for, expected (or even wanted) in so many churches.* We typically make no place for His real presence or His freedom to move unhindered in our midst! Unfortunately, when we ever do make any efforts in this direction, they are often ridiculously short and surface. Though God is awesomely powerful and can certainly force His will in our midst, He generally chooses to move when He is invited and given the freedom to manifest His presence. It is little wonder His glorious presence is so rare in most congregations!

While I am in *no way* advocating disorder, emotionalism or sloppiness, it is utterly essential that we embrace more Spirit-sensitivity and less human micro-managing. It is essential that we at least provide the "opportunity" and guidance for people to deeply encounter God. Furthermore, I strongly stress such patterns are *not* impractical or unachievable in modern churches! Even formal somewhat stiff churches can learn to encounter God. To those who desire His real presence and power, God will surely give balance and wisdom to keep things "proper and in order."

In our day, it is extremely urgent that we again learn to seek and embrace God's manifest presence. We must hunger and settle for nothing less than experiencing "God Himself" not just services "about" Him. Giving time and encouragement for people to encounter God is indeed a desperate need for modern congregations. Revivals and genuine power never come by tight bondage to clocks or human orchestration. Addressing this need is paramount in today's Church!

30. *Many churches became more programmed and formula-focused than genuinely God-centered and Spirit-guided in receiving His unique vision for them. Rather than truly seeking and hearing God themselves, they merely plug in the latest program, fad or book study. Unfortunately, there are no "short-cuts" to true revival or deep intimacy with Christ.*

Beyond question, great power and historic revivals come from deeply prayerful, Spirit-guided churches, not mere programs and formulas. While biblical programs and formulas have great value and should be prayerfully utilized, they can also become a subtle substitute for closely seeking God. If all we do is plug in programs and book studies, we can become spiritually lazy and fail to seriously seek God for ourselves. Though there are indeed basic purposes and principles that are always applicable, God's specific vision for each church has a beautiful uniqueness. Beyond question, God typically has at least some unique instructions, ministries and timing for each congregation. Yet if churches simply plug in the latest program, they can easily become more human-orchestrated than truly God-centered and Spirit-guided.

Believers, we must never forget God's great desire is for each believer and church to walk with Him in deep intimacy, faith and kingdom mission. And while God may well lead churches to use many of today's quality studies and tools, there is almost always at least "some" uniqueness of application beyond the program. God desires individual intimacy and specific vision for each believer and church, not cookie-cutter formulas. If we are truly listening, He often leads into paths that are unique in living out the Acts 1:8 Great Commission. True New Testament power comes from leaders and churches that walk in profound closeness, prayerful surrender and the specific faith of a God-given vision.

God Desires Intimacy and Uniqueness With Each Church
"Getting *God's* Vision Not Just *Our* Plans"

In Scripture and revival history, it is hard to miss an incredible uniqueness in how God guides His people from task to task. In Scripture, God's guidance and timing was usually very detailed and specific to each different group. While foundational principles *never* varied, method and timing *often* did. The same is true of history's great revivals. Though they all had certain foundational elements, each revival also had its uniqueness. Given these facts, why do so many churches do little or nothing beyond set, pre-packaged programs? This tendency is a likely reason many see so little in terms of major growth and lasting impact.

Again let me stress the preceding observations in no way suggest biblical programs are unworthy. No doubt, there is real value in solid tools. Biblical strategies and scriptural book studies can often help us stay focused on essential foundational purposes. Yet if leaders and churches settle for working rigid programs and strategies, they may never fervently pray and seek God themselves. In light of today's extreme spiritual urgency, churches simply *must* return to deep intimacy and specific instruction from God Himself.

In my decades of pastoral experience, seeking God's specific vision was *absolutely key* to a miraculous expansion of church ministries! Each year, we prayerfully sought God's church-wide direction and vision for the coming months. He nearly always revealed something new and challenging. As a direct result, God gave a most unlikely, challenged church a publishing ministry into many nations and a radio ministry reaching several states. But above all, we experienced the indescribable joy of discovering God's unique vision for our church. I again stress that *any* church can learn to receive a clear, detailed vision from our Lord. By "vision" I don't mean coming up with our own plans and asking God to bless them. I mean diligently seeking God for His vision!

No generation has ever so widely embraced programs, book studies and formulas as has ours. If tools, programs, formulas and book studies (alone) could bring sweeping revival, we would have long since had the largest in history. Instead, we have had the exact opposite! The fact we need more than cookie-cutter approaches should be completely obvious to all. Yet even now, a growing number of leaders are awakening to these very truths. There is a dawning realization we're not going to program, promote, strategize or talk our way into a Great spiritual Awakening. At last, millions are hungering for God Himself! And while we should thank God for quality strategies and utilize biblical tools, let us even more seek God for the uniqueness of our own vision. Only that kind of closeness and vision can avert and reverse the spiritual disaster directly in our path.

31. *Classic signs of biblical judgment have rapidly increased and loom very heavy on the near horizon.*

> *America and the western Church now have virtually all of the key biblical indicators of likely judgment from God. By many indicators, we have already come through several stages of judgment and are on the edge of far worse.*

As we observe the many instances of judgment in the Bible, it is wholly apparent that God's dealings follow very consistent patterns.[61] Currently, we are seeing these distinct indicators on every hand. Even the most casual understanding of biblical patterns suggests gravest concern for conditions in America and the western Church. As seldom (if ever) in our history, we are witnessing a rapid and unusual "convergence" of ominous signs from many directions.

Yet for balance, let me quickly state not all current signs are bad and there is evidence at least "some" of God's protective hand is still in place (though that could change in an instant.) Let me also state not all of the signs I mention necessarily indicate direct judgment. Attacks, difficulties and trials do not always equate to direct judgment from God. And indeed, God could yet decide to show mercy for an extended time.

Believe me, I am fully aware "crying judgment" can be slippery slope and well-meaning people are often wrong. It can also be risky to start attributing this or that event to "judgment" while ignoring others. By so doing, people have attributed things to God that He did not do. Make no mistake — it is profoundly dangerous to misrepresent holy God. We'd better be dead sure before any of us start popping off about the exact details and timing of God's judgments.

However, I strongly believe there are unprecedented distinctives to many of the signs we will examine under this point. The "sudden convergence" of so many factors is most unusual and highly suggestive of increasing judgment. As to the question of whether we "might" be under judgment, the more appropriate question is how could we *not* be under judgment (given today's appalling morals and blatant rebellion?) While it is still possible God could graciously protect and send revival, current times are unquestionably very urgent. Millions of praying people have an internal sense that "something big is coming." While only God knows details of the what, when and how, believers must be alert to His patterns of biblical judgment. We are not to be sleeping or clueless about the "signs of our times." (Matthew 16:1-3) It is time for us to sound the warning and call people back to true surrender to Jesus.

Recognizing the Biblical "Patterns" of God's Judgment
We Must Not Be Blind or Silent!
(Ezekiel 33:6-7)

There comes a time when God's hand is so clear, His people must not be blind and deaf. After all, God has pledged to give His servants key insights into His activity. *"Surely the Lord GOD does nothing, Unless He reveals His secret to His servants the prophets."* (Amos 3:7; John 15:15; 1 Thessalonians 5:1-5) Now is the time to strongly "suspect" and "prepare for" the possibility of increasing judgments! In my own heart, it has moved from "suspecting" to "expecting." (Although I also expect a revival among God's remnant.) Indeed two key purposes of this book are: (a) *to prepare believers to return to God and hopefully avoid the severest judgments*, or (b) *to seek God and understand His judgments if and when they are fully unleashed.*

Current signs of gathering judgment demand our deepest attention and prayerful repentance. Especially if serious trials begin to fall, we need to be aware of God's patterns and ways in judgment. After all, God's people are to "walk in the light" and have understanding into His activity. (John 15:15; 1 Thessalonians 5:1-5) Though we likely won't know all details and times, mature saints should not be asleep or blind-sided by God's major acts. By God's indwelling Spirit, we are to have eyes to see the clear signs of His activity. Especially when they are as obvious as today! The very essence of spiritual leadership is to be able to discern and interpret God's will and proclaim His message to the Church and nation. In other words, it is crucial that preachers and leaders boldly warn believers of rising judgment and call them to return to God.

God's Patience is Not Endless!
"Stages, Pauses and Opportunities" in God's Judgment
(Exodus 7-12; Isaiah 5:1-7; Amos 4:6-13)

Biblically when God brings judgment, He generally does it in distinct "stages." His mercy is so great, God often increases judgments gradually because He so deeply desires people to receive His correction and repent. Yet, His holiness demands that persistent willful sin be judged. Our Lord usually brings stages of judgment that intensify if people ignore His warnings.

God's stages of judgment often include any or all of three elements: (1) a progressive lessening of divine protection and blessing, (2) raising up enemies and (3) allowing (or sending) various catastrophes and trials. (Isaiah 5:1-7; Amos 4:6-13; Luke 19:42-44) It is also true that God usually judges or strikes a people at two places in particular: (a) the points of their greatest strengths or pride, (b) the most treasured idols of their hearts (i.e. money, sex, power, recreation, etc.) His corrections and judgment typically *target* primary areas of idolatry and fleshly reliance!

At the various stages of increasing judgment, there are typically "pauses" at which time God sends more prophetic words and warnings. Normally, there are key moments of God-given "opportunity" for His people (or sinful nations) to respond. We see this in Jesus' sad lament over the fact Israel did not realize the time of their "visitation" (or opportunity) to respond to God's invitation for peace. Because they neglected such a crucial day of visitation," they would be utterly destroyed. (Luke 19:42-44) The degree of judgment is often related to the size of the opportunity. What could be worse than rejecting Jesus face to face? Since America has long enjoyed unusual blessing, supernatural protection and enormous opportunity to hear His word, we too stand in danger of severest judgment.

Make no mistake — we respond when God calls or we don't respond at all. There indeed comes a point for individuals, churches or nations when it is simply "too late." In Scripture, it is very clear that an attempted response of obedience *after* God's appointed time is fruitless, futile and in some cases disastrous. (Numbers 14:39-45; Proverbs 29:1; Jeremiah 14:19-5:4; Hebrews 12:17) Saints, we must never trifle with God's invitations or take for granted we have plenty of time to repent! Only God knows the moment when we cross His line and go too far.

God's Judgment is Precise and Targeted, Not Arbitrary

As we study God's judgment throughout Scripture, it is very clear His actions are with purpose and precise justice. God's judgments are typically correlated to the type of offense or the particular "idol of the heart." Some examples include: (1) The children of Israel continually complaining and accusing God of "bringing them into the wilderness to kill them. As a result, God caused them to wander until they actually did die in the wilderness. (Numbers 14:1-25) (2) Acting on Gods' behalf, Moses requiring Israel to drink the ground up false idol they had worshipped. (3) Because David used the enemy's sword to kill Uriah and take his wife, the sword would never depart from David's house and their wives would be taken by enemies (2 Samuel 12:9-15) (4) God took David's beloved son because David had taken the beloved wife of Uriah and had him murdered. (2 Samuel 12:16-22) (5) Israel forsook God and worshipped alien gods in their own land so now they would be enslaved by aliens in a land not theirs. (Jeremiah 5:18) (6) Sins of physical immorality and irreverence often bring judgment upon the physical body. (Romans 1:27; 1 Corinthians 11:27-32) In many ways, Galatians 6:7 sums up patterns of judgment as well as the consequences of persistent sins. *"Do not be deceived, God is not mocked; for **whatever** a man sows, **that** he will also reap."*

In light of biblical patterns, it is quite obvious America's central idols of the heart are materialism, pride, self will, greed, immorality, perversion, blasphemous irreverence and lost fear of God. Thus if God fully judges America and many churches, it will likely be at the point of our money, pride and power. Severe economic and national setbacks would strike at the heart of our idolatry and pride. May God help us repent and fully realize, "We are not invulnerable!" It would be well to remember the words of Dr. Adrian Rogers. "God's judgment grinds *slowly* but it grinds *surely* and *finely.*" Dear saints, God's promise is not endless and His judgments are sure. (Numbers 32:23)

The Shift from "Remedial" to Catastrophic" Judgments
*"He who is often rebuked, and hardens his neck, Will **suddenly** be destroyed, and that **without remedy.**"(Proverbs 29:1)*

If God's people respond and genuinely repent, the judgments eventually cease and blessing returns. (Though sometimes even in repentance, consequences may for a period remain or even worsen.) Even though God forgives the sin (when confessed and forsaken) in some cases the earthly consequences must long endure. If however the people ignore God's voice, His judgment continues in ever-increasing intensity. There is then often something of a turning point when God's judgment "suddenly" moves from *remedial* to the *catastrophic* and *punitive.* (Proverbs 29:1)

For clarification, "remedial" judgments are generally a series of escalating conditions or events designed to get believers' attention to correct their behavior and turn their hearts back to God. These judgments are more "redemptive" (or remedial) in their intended purpose. Such judgments are somewhat designed to awaken and correct. They are typically tempered with considerable mercy. Conversely, catastrophic (or punitive) judgments are more about destruction and punishment. They are much more severe and typically longer lasting. For certain individuals or groups, they may well be permanent. Yet even in these, God does not wholly abandon His true saints.

Concerning this point, readers should be fore-warned. Once God indeed moves from remedial to catastrophic judgment, the devastation is generally severe and long-lasting. It crosses a point and becomes irrevocable. Please listen to His strong warning. *"God will judge **His** people"* and *"it is a fearful thing to fall into the hands of the living God."* (Hebrews 10:30-31)

It is profoundly sobering to realize there are times God says it is "too late" even though we may try to respond. (Numbers 14:39-45; Jeremiah 14:19-15:4) There are definitely times God tell His prophets, *"Therefore **do not pray** for this people, nor lift up a cry or prayer for them, nor make intercession to Me; for I will not hear you."* (Jeremiah 7:16) Readers should remember they are times when it was "too late" for those who had crossed the line of grace. Even now some reading these words are likely right on the line. I believe this book may well be a last choice for many persons, churches and denominations. It is surely not an accident you are reading these words at that precise moment. I beg you to immediately fall on your knees and cry out to God for full repentance!

Judgment "Begins" with God's People
"For the time has come for judgment to begin at the house of God; and if it begins with us first, what will be the end of those who do not obey the gospel of God?"
(1 Peter 4:17)

Believers, we must fully understand that judgment *"begins* at the house of God." (1 Peter 4:17) Rather than blaming lost society, we should realize God heals the land if *His* people seriously humble themselves, pray and repent. (2 Chronicles 7:14) To me, it is very clear both America and many churches have blown past one warning after another.

The fact we are saturated with Bible preaching further increases our accountability. Even though some might claim "we haven't heard God's warnings," it certainly wasn't for lack of opportunity. There is nothing sadder than individuals, churches or nations that miss their day of "visitation" (or opportunity) to hear and respond to God. (Luke 19:44) I believe we may well be in our very last opportunity to hear and repent. For greater clarity and urgency, prayerfully consider ten factors that strongly suggest a present lessening of divine protection and increasing levels of active judgment. While most of these signs are right out of Scripture, a couple also come from historic patterns of nations on the verge of major decline. With nearly fifty million abortions, the exaltation of perversion, rampant abominations and exploding blasphemies, we can only tremble at America's fearsome accountability before holy God. The following ten factors indeed suggest a fast approaching spiritual iceberg. The iceberg consists of sin's inevitable laws of reaping and God's righteous judgment. (Galatians 6:7-9)

Ten Signs of Imminent Judgment
The Biblical and Social Warning Signs

(1) *America and many churches have moved far into the two primary conditions that bring an extremely heightened risk for destructive consequences and judgment.* (Jeremiah 2:4-13; Luke 12:47-48; Proverbs 29:1; Hebrews 10:26) Risk for judgment is always far higher for individuals, churches and nations that fit the following two categories. (a) They blatantly sin and reject God though He has blessed and favored them in unusual ways. *"To whom much is given, much is required."* (Jeremiah 2:4-13; Luke 12:48) (b) They continue in willful sin though they have had great exposure to God's word and received many warnings. In other words, they continue in sin though they have had full opportunity to know God's will. There is far more accountability to those who are fully aware of God's instruction. (Proverbs 29:1; Luke 12:47; Hebrews 10:26)

On both counts, America and the Western Church have *fearsome accountability* and much heightened risk before God! Indeed, no nation on earth (besides Israel) is even close to having had such unusual favor and protection from God. It is even unquestionably true that some of our national documents amounted to a type of "covenant" to trust in God and exalt Christ as Lord. Even our very currency says "In God We Trust." America has also had unequalled exposure to His Word and truth.

In light of God's phenomenal blessings and America's blatant and innumerable abominations, it is frankly astounding He has not already sent catastrophic judgment. In a very real sense, America has repeatedly spit in the face of Holy God! We have done despite to His grace and mocked His holiness. Given our incredibly generous blessings and repeated opportunities, we must *tremble* at our potential for severe judgment. (Jeremiah 5:22) I believe there are strong signs we are in our very last moments of opportunity for mercy. In fact, we may well have already crossed the line! And yet, even in judgment there is hope *if* we fully repent.

(2) *Statistics show a significant majority of churches are spiritually weak and virtually powerless to turn today's rushing tide of evil.* (Number 14:39-45; Joshua 7:1-13; 2 Chronicles 6:24) We should clearly note that a major sign of judgment is spiritual weakness and a conspicuous absence of God's manifest glory and power among His people. Jesus said, hells gates will not prevail against the Church. Again, this is a picture of the Church on the offensive, not retreating in defeat! (Matthew 16:18) The fact an astonishing 70-80 percent of American churches are plateaued or declining is complete proof God's full face of blessing is turned away (from most.)

Even the baptism patterns of today's so-called "successful" churches seriously pale beside the awesome power of revival generations. They also pale beside the patterns of some current churches in Africa, China, India, Korea and parts of South America. While churches being under persecution is not necessarily a sign of judgment, churches in severe spiritual apathy and weakness *are* clear signs of God's departed glory. When societies' churches become weak and compromised, societies soon begin to experience the tragic conditions described under the next point.

(3) *The last twenty years represent by far our severest collapse of morals and family life. We have also witnessed a catastrophic decline in the numbers that hold a biblical world view. Vast numbers have lost any fear and reverence for God, His word or His work.* "If the foundations are destroyed, what can the righteous do?" (Psalms 11:3) Make no mistake — when the reverential fear of God leaves a people, they have moved into a whole new realm of decline and judgment. When they no longer believe sin brings accountability and consequences, a significant line has been crossed! As a result, we have suffered

an explosive proliferation of perversion, occult, psychics, moral relativism and radical false religions. A literal belief in Scriptural authority has plummeted. This condition fully sets the stage for the evil conditions just before many of God's severest judgments.

At this point, America's spiritual climate has raced far beyond basic immorality. We are a society increasingly filled with "unnatural affections," perversion, child pornography and false religions. The Bible gives a profound and sobering pronouncement to societies in such severe spiritual collapse. God says these are signs of a society He has "given over" to extreme depravity and "unnatural desires." (Romans 1:20-30) Such patterns describe a society in very advanced stages of judgment. According to Scripture, any such society is headed for catastrophic judgment and internal social collapse. (Proverbs 14:34) Another historic spiritual awakening is the only hope of change.

(4) *Today, we are witnessing an astoundingly rapid proliferation of highly motivated, empowered political, social, economic and religious enemies.* (Isaiah 5:1-7; Jeremiah 1:13-16; 6:19-23) Though enemies, sickness or trials certainly don't always mean God's direct judgment, when accompanied by an unusually rapid and severe moral collapse, they are highly suggestive of such. Throughout Scripture, a major form of judgment is a marked increase of emboldened, wicked enemies whose attacks are more or less successful. (Isaiah 5:1-7; Jeremiah 6:19-23) Considering 9/11, massive natural disasters and many developing geo-political hostilities, it seems clear God is withholding at least some of the hedge with which He once sheltered America and her churches. (Isaiah 5:1-7)

Although our nation has experienced worse trials than the current, we have never been so saturated with blasphemy and perversion. Again, while enemies and trials certainly do not always mean direct judgment, our appalling state of moral and spiritual collapse make current developments very suspicious. Seldom have so many immoral, religious and geo-political forces "simultaneously converged' from without and within. Rogue nations and sworn enemies are increasingly getting weapons of mass destruction. (And currently we seem mostly unable to stop it.) Even many of the nation's schools and universities are now bastions of extreme anti-American, anti-Christian propaganda. Obviously, this severely blinds and poisons the minds of millions who will soon govern our land.

Growing forces of social evil have declared war on everything from "Christmas" and the "Pledge of Allegiance" to "In God We Trust" on our currency. At present, cults, false religions and atheists frequently have more media prestige than the evangelical Church. False religions are often being given more privileges and deference than Christians. Again, when we see the rapid advancement of evil forces and rapid decline of righteousness, we know God's hand is withheld from His Church. Victorious churches prevail — backslidden churches retreat! (Mathew 16:18) Perhaps even more telling is the fact we have now gone far longer without a Great Awakening than any previous period in American history. It is most conspicuous and unusual that we are so badly over due for a heaven-sent sweeping revival. Given all the above factors, it would be spiritually irresponsible *not* to suspect God's righteous judgment.

(5) *We now see the election of increasingly immoral, anti-Christian leaders who will do or say anything to get elected.* (Isaiah 5:20; Jeremiah 5:30-31) Many politicians blatantly pander to any group that might give them a vote. With these traitorous leaders, what is good for the long-term viability of the country has no bearing — it is all about protecting their own political careers. It is about advancing the "political party" far more than the good of overall society. Recently, many forms of politics and "political correctness" have delved into the realm

of sheer lunacy. With so many self-destructive policies and trends, our country is literally committing suicide. Society is unquestionably in a spiritual freefall of "calling good evil and evil good." (Isaiah 5:20)

What is even more disgusting (and transparent) is the way these godless political candidates claim to be "Christian" and have a significant "personal faith." Yet with so many, they have never attended church with regularity and have personal lifestyles wholly inconsistent with Christ's teachings. They support the most obviously immoral causes yet say "my Christian faith is important to me." Not only is this obviously designed to get votes, it is also a very real form of blasphemous mockery. It is utterly wicked for someone to try and falsely use religion to get "Christian votes" while supporting all that is immoral and ungodly. This is a clear sign of people past any fear of God and a society "given over" to utter depravity. (Romans 1:28)

Tragically, many politicians are actually leading the charge in today's plunge off the moral, social and spiritual cliff. Surveys make clear the moral, social and policy views of elected leaders have dramatically changed (for the worse) in just ten short years. Worse yet, many of the candidates on the political horizon are even *far* less Christian, moral (or even American) in their views and practices. Make no mistake — a *major* sign of judgment is when God hands His people over to leaders who are godless, self-serving and foolish. Even now, we are seeing a profound (and disturbing) shift in the beliefs and practices of today's political candidates. This negative shift is an extremely ominous indicator of increasing judgment. God may well be "giving us over" to worsening depravity. (Romans 1:20-32) When He hands His people over to increasingly ungodly leaders, it nearly always signals a far more serious phase of judgment.

(6) *Currently, there is serious confusion and seeming irrationality among many religious, government and financial leaders.* (Job 12:20-25; Jeremiah 5:30-31; Micah 3:1-8) Seldom have so many government, religious and financial institutions seemed to flounder and lack clear direction. Many now seem seriously lacking in the backbone and wisdom to stand strong against evil. A major sign of biblical judgment is rampant immorality, confusion and poor decisions among religions and government leaders. Some of the things our government now allows (and defends) is absurd to the extreme.

Today, many politicians and judges do not even have the common sense to recognize (or care) that deadly enemies are twisting our laws to their own wicked purposes. For so many in leadership, plain common sense and reason have long since vanished. It seems the good leaders are more and more outnumbered by the bad. When God judges His people, He allows them to have leaders that are self-serving and unwise. (Micah 3:1-8)

(7) *Today we are witnessing an unprecedented explosion of political and religious scandals.* (Jeremiah 23:9-15) Not only are the scandals more numerous, they are far more brazen and perverted. Worse yet, the society is so depraved it doesn't even matter. In so many cases, they get elected anyway! While there are indeed "some" good leaders we should certainly *support* and *encourage*, they are often so outnumbered there is often little they can do. In judgment, the efforts of the righteous are often blocked and sabotaged by self-serving partisanship. Today, we should be soberly aware no one sees (and is encouraged) by our political wrangling more than American's deadly enemies. It is further ominous to realize God often gives people the leaders they deserve. (Jeremiah 5:30-31) How sobering to realize a free society generally elects leaders in its "own image."

(8) *At present, our nation is plunging toward massive infrastructure crises of our own making.* Our land is in a devastating drought of common sense and wisdom. (Job 12:20-25; Jeremiah 4:22; Hosea 4:6) Today everywhere we look, we see problems that arise from plain self-interest on the part of politicians. Of special concern are the ominous signs and unusual occurrence in the now highly interconnected American and global financial markets. Other key examples of infrastructure and financial signs are: excessive energy dependence, Medicare and Social Security bankruptcy, floods of illegal aliens, runaway budget deficits, crashing value of the dollar, mortgage and lending crisis, etc. Each of the above issues is a major crises all by themselves. Yet, all of these converging at the same time are a potential "perfect storm" or tsunami of financial pain. It is also again significant that God's judgment typically strikes at the "central root" of our false idols. In America, these are unquestionably the gods of money, immorality, pride, self-sufficiency and pleasure seeking. An economic collapse would hit the very heart of our central false god!

In essence all of the above crises could have been solved with relative ease if addressed early. Good judgment, common sense and timely action would have long ago fixed most (if not all) of our current internal crises. Yet, they have been passed from decade to decade with self-serving political gamesmanship. When we look at many of today's decisions and policies, it truly seems "the inmates are running the asylum." On an unprecedented number of fronts, there are gathering clouds of serious social crises.

(9) *Through lack of moral will, politics and sheer foolishness, modern leaders have ignored national border integrity until it has become a desperate, fast worsening crisis.* (Job 12:20-25; Jeremiah 4:22) We are only now beginning to see the coming wave of heinous crimes by millions of illegal

alien criminals added to our already huge domestic criminal population (though certainly not all illegal aliens are violent criminals.) Even after years of watching a raging flood of illegal aliens, they are still pouring in like a river. (And all in a time of extreme terrorist threat.) The nation is literally being inundated with illegals, terrorists and criminals. Only God knows how many are terrorist cells and religious radicals. In a day of unparalleled high risk, current policies border on insanity and national suicide. Historically, one of the final signs of a nation in moral, social and political collapse is when it can't (or won't) even enforce its own national borders.

(10) *We have witnessed a disturbing rise in unusually devastating natural and human-caused disasters with far worse potential on the immediate horizon.* (2 Chronicles 6:24-28) From a wide variety of angles, the stage is uniquely set for severe potential judgment. In the last five years alone, we have seen unusually intense hurricanes, ominous signs from dormant seismic faults, unprecedented wildfires, droughts, floods, virulent highly organized terrorists (with increasing access to a variety of weapons of mass destruction) and looming infrastructure crises. In speaking with many of our disaster relief teams, most report more serious natural disasters in the last five years than the twenty immediately prior. Seldom (if ever) in history have we seen so many disasters of so many different kinds with such severity.

Today a vastly increased risk is the unprecedented new development and proliferation of biological and chemical agents. Deadly enemies have ever-increasing access to ever-evolving weapons. The nuclear, biological, chemical and financial genie is more out of the bottle everyday. While technology has brought blessings, it has also brought an explosion of vastly more harmful (and now more deliverable) threats into the wrong hands. When enemies are gladly willing to blow themselves up, it opens whole new levels of attack for which we have little effective defense. The "potential" for harm is suddenly much greater.

We are also witnessing strange, unprecedented developments in the nation's monetary and stock systems. In so many parts of the new global electronic economy, we are in totally uncharted waters. Everything is so new and fast-moving, there are dangers that give financial experts many sleepless nights. From so many directions, clouds of potential judgment have seldom been more numerous or threatening. Make no mistake — if God wanted to quickly judge and utterly humble America, the means are now fully in place. All of the above are foreboding signs of looming judgment if we do not repent with great sincerity and thoroughness. (2 Chronicles 7:12-14)

Do You Now Sense God's Call to Repentance?
A Most Urgent Wake Up Call!

It is again important to note that every single one of the above factors reflect a classic sign that often accompanied biblical judgment! While some would say it is possible all of this happening at once is just a "coincidence," I do not believe that is the case. Only profound ignorance of Scripture and history could allow one to remain glib in the face of today's unparalleled developments that are so rapidly worsening.

Indeed the most troubling sign is the sudden "simultaneous convergence" of so many evil factors with profound political, religious and social implications. Think about it — people are now getting elected to public office that wouldn't have had a chance just ten years ago (become of gross immorality, perversion or support of the same.) The nation now seems poised to dive even far deeper in these directions. It is also abundantly clear that few have seriously turned to God despite many "wake up calls." Believers, if the events of 9/11 barely got our attention (spiritually), we have to wonder what it *would* take to seriously humble us before God? If we don't fully repent and seek God by His appointed means, *we will soon find out!*

Any suggestion that "God doesn't judge today" or that "it couldn't happen to us" is dangerously out of touch with biblical teaching. Whether or not it is politically correct or popular, I am duty bound to proclaim "God *does* judge and its signs abound on every hand!" The Bible leaves no doubt that God indeed judges both people and nations that continually reject His Word and will. (Especially when they have been unusually blessed and heavily exposed to His Word.) In Scripture, God typically sent progressive, remedial warnings before His judgment became cataclysmic. But one thing is certain — God cannot ignore blatant sin and blasphemy indefinitely.

We Are *Not* Invulnerable!

Do we really think an extended, nation-wide drought or a series of massive earthquakes, a terrorist's dirty bomb or economic collapse is impossible? Do we think we are invulnerable? If so, we should think again and ask forgiveness for such a dangerous and irrational arrogance. If God so chooses, He could in fact allow all of the above scenarios and many others to occur at one time. Indeed, we are *not* invulnerable! By blatant arrogance and continuing sin, we could force the same God Who raised us up to now bring us down.

Dear saints, our loving, gracious God does not judge quickly or willingly. (Lamentations 3:33) Yet when His people remain proud and blatantly unrepentant, after many warnings and clear instruction, God's full judgment often falls "suddenly." (Proverbs 29:1) When their prayers and repentance remained surface, half-hearted and token, God's holiness *required* strong biblical judgment. The wheels of God's judgment often grind slowly but they grind *surely*. Readers should fully understand that several unprecedented factors are in place that could bring our society to its knees in very rapid fashion. Even now, geo-political factors, demographics, spiritual enemies, terrorists and natural disasters are uniquely poised for potential devastation beyond anything we have seen in modern times.

For several years, we have seen increasing classic signs of rising remedial judgments on our churches and society. While there may yet be hope of returning to God and avoiding full judgment, multiple signs point to profound urgency (and extreme lateness) of the hour. Far greater emphases on repentance and God-seeking prayer are the only hope of a Great Awakening. Yet, instead of broken contrition, intense solemn assemblies and urgent priority focus, most still give only peripheral lip-service to prayer, holiness and repentance.

Are We At Last Ready to Seriously Repent?
(Or Continue "Painting Chairs" on the Titanic?)

Many churches and conventions still proceed as if better programs, slicker slogans or harder promotions can somehow turn this massive tide of evil. Frankly such an attitude is as futile as busily *"painting deck chairs on the Titanic"* (just after it hit the iceberg.) In light of Scripture and current realities, any idea of just "staying the same course that got us here" is not only ridiculous, it is spiritually traitorous. It is the very epitome of declaring "smooth words" and "peace" in the face of coming disaster.

Leaders, make no mistake — it is our primary responsibility to tell the whole truth both about our real condition and potential coming judgments. We must shout God's primary message of urgency and repentance. *If the "watchman" don't clearly shout the alarm, who will?"* (Ezekiel 3:17; 33:6) Leaders, if we don't loudly proclaim God's central message of deep repentance and purity, our hands are red with the blood of this generation! (Ezekiel 33:8)

Believers, if there is to be any real hope, our priorities concerning prayer, repentance and evangelism must immediately change! Make no mistake — it is time for godly leaders to arise, sound the alarm and provide clear direction. We don't need any more rhetoric or temporary surface events, we need strong specific action and changed foundational patterns! Neither do we need men who merely preach — we need leaders who are *examples* of profound brokenness, holiness, prayer and fasting. Pastors and prayer leaders who don't personally pray, weep and fast will have little power in calling others to do so. While this does not mean all leaders must daily pray three or four hours to be used of God, it does mean we must all move beyond brief, shallow and tearless devotions. But by God's grace, we *can* do this. Leaders, it is time! In fact it is at least forty years past time. We must fully humble ourselves and *"seek the Lord while He may yet be found."* (Isaiah 55:6)

What Keeps Leaders Silent?
"Recapturing Biblical Boldness and Clarity"
(Ezekiel 33:7; 1 Corinthians 14:8)

In the next chapter, we will discuss issues that could keep leaders from changing "enough" to truly miss the spiritual iceberg. As busy people our great danger is three-fold. (1) That we would essentially *ignore* true conditions and just keep following the same basic patterns. (2) That we would acknowledge an urgent need for change but simply *delay* getting serious about making any. (3) That we would make minor changes that *do not go far enough* to bring revival. Leadership is definitely going to be the central key to true repentance and revival.

I urge every leader to give special attention to the next chapter. It helps us see the subtle ways we could unintentionally miss our crucial opportunity. Indeed, our enemy is a master at keeping us from getting serious about meaningful change. Please pause and pray for clear insight on our true conditions and necessary preparations for powerful repentance.

A Time for Leaders to Lead
Watchman Sound the Alarm!

"Repentance or Judgment"

"But if the watchman sees the sword coming and does not blow the trumpet, and the people are not warned, and the sword comes and takes any person from among them, he is taken away in his iniquity; but his blood I will require at the watchman's hand.' "So you, son of man: I have made you a watchman for the house of Israel; therefore you shall hear a word from My mouth and warn them for Me." (Ezekiel 33:6-7)

"If the trumpeter sounds an uncertain note, who will prepare for battle?" (1 Corinthians 14:8)

Chapter Four

It's Time for Leaders to Lead!
"Repentance or Decline and Judgment"

As we have clearly seen in preceding chapters, the American Church and nation are at a crucial crossroad of unparalleled importance! Never has so vast an array of demographic, social and spiritual factors uniquely "converged" to create a pivotal moment of such staggering implications. It is like a "perfect storm" of wicked influence and evil impact. Because of the breath-taking speed of changes, cultural and religious patterns are now entering a most dangerous period of transition. While a few denominations have been able to stave off serious decline, most are experiencing unprecedented stagnation and loss.[68] For most groups, baptism ratios are at all-time lows.

The few that have shown growth have by no means kept pace with population percentages. Furthermore, some of what is now being called "growth" is neither balanced nor biblical. Especially disturbing is the fact today's rapidly increasing moral collapse is actually worse in the Bible belt! Never have so many elaborate religious programs and aggressive promotions produced so little actual societal impact. Beyond question, the present hour calls for profound spiritual adjustments, not a little improvement or re-packaging of current programs. Clearly, we cannot merely throw in a little "token" prayer, "casual" repentance or "new slogans" and expect massive change.

A Cycle of "Exponentially" Increasing Evil

Of even far greater concern is the fact social and spiritual changes are moving into a cycle of much more rapid escalation. In such a pattern negative changes do not simply increase, they begin to explode *exponentially!* When this occurs, evil factors are cumulative and reach a deadly point of critical mass. At that juncture, widespread societal impact multiplies with astonishing speed. Severe evil effects then become much like a snowball tumbling down a hill. The further it goes, the larger it grows and faster it moves! Make no mistake — we are right at that point. Because of an unusual "convergence of factors," we are fast moving toward even far greater changes.

One of many examples is the serious demographic "age bomb" soon to hit churches and denominations with devastating force. The high percentages of churches now heavily attended and founded by seniors will rapidly shrink as millions of their members soon die. Without another huge Awakening, we will almost surely suffer conditions *much* worse than the present moral collapse. Saints, we are far past being much helped by better methods and strategies alone. Only a massive, God-sent revival can turn this raging tide.

Europe's Spiritual Collapse
"A Sobering Object Lesson for America"

If any believers still need convincing, all they need do is look at the shocking spiritual conditions of modern Europe. It is extremely sobering to realize not so long ago, Europe was the central source of most Great Awakenings and virtually all Christian denominations. Until shortly before 1900, Europe was also a predominant source of world mission efforts. Yet just a little over a hundred years later, only a tiny percentage of Europeans ever even attend church (much less sponsor missionaries.) The few who do attend do so in churches that are mostly ritualistic, un-evangelistic and spiritually dead. Worse yet, of the very small percentages of Europeans who attend church, the overwhelming number of them are older senior adults soon to depart this life.

In today's Europe, several cults and false religions flourish while evangelical churches continue their downward spiral. At this point the European culture is not only predominantly secular, it is largely anti-God in its worldview.[69] It is truly shocking to realize how quickly whole nations can move from revival passion to an almost militant paganism. Any idea this could not happen to America is naïve, biblically ignorant and dangerously arrogant.

Will America Go the Way of Europe?

The devastating spiritual collapse of Europe should instill a profound reverential fear of the God Who spares no nation that turns its back on His truth. In both Testaments, God gave sober warnings to His own people who persistently abandoned or neglected His ways. (2 Chronicles 7:12-22; Revelation 2:1-3:17) Frankly, it is shocking that any believers would actually suggest God no longer sends judgments. Those who say God no longer judges sin know very little about the Old and New Testaments. Both Testaments are replete with teachings of sin's accountability and God's sure judgment. Contrary to some of today's shallow, unbiblical views of God, His grace is neither cheap nor limitless! When the churches of a land remain blatantly self-focused, lukewarm, proud or compromised, God in time surely shifts His primary anointing to other nations. Any idea the "age of grace" means God is "light on sin" is completely contrary to New Testament teachings. (Acts 5:1-5; 1 Corinthians 11:26-32; Hebrews 10:26-31; 1 Peter 4:17; Revelation 2:1-3:15)

Though God is incredibly loving, His holiness *requires* eventual judgment on churches that long continue in blatant apathy and sin. According to Revelation Chapters 2-3, part of God's judgment is to remove His manifest blessing and power from such churches (referred to as removing their "candlestick.") When this occurs, churches languish in weakness and many close their doors. Removing a candlestick can also certainly mean that particular congregation dies (or is destroyed.) It is sobering to realize God is under no necessary obligation to restore the candlestick to any person, church or nation.

A little over a century ago, God clearly turned His primary ministry activity from the churches of Europe to those of America. Indeed, vast numbers of Europe's churches no longer exist and many of those remaining are desperately weak and rapidly dying.[70]

Yet today, there are increasingly ominous signs for America. The great majority of American churches are declining or stagnant while churches in China, Korea and India explode with New Testament power.[71] Churches in China and Korea are now actually sending missionaries to America! (Because so many in our nation are unchurched and most churches are so dead and weak.) In light of current conditions, certain questions cry out for answers.

Is God Turning Now His Face from America?
"The Most Urgent Questions of the Hour"

Because of the devastating declines in church strength and national morals, we are driven to ponder several sobering questions. Are we indeed beginning to see a major spiritual shift as so many American churches decline and die while the persecuted churches of other lands experience phenomenal growth? Could God now be turning from America to pour His greatest anointing on other lands? Is there still a chance for America to seriously repent and avert far worse decline and collapse? Can we again see historic revival and spiritual awakening sweep our land? Is there really any hope for a society so far advanced in apathy, perversion and compromise? If so, exactly what must we do to seriously return to God? Why have so many quality programs and promotions utterly failed to bring sweeping revival? What can we change to reverse these disturbing patterns? Alas, these are the burning questions that overshadow all others.

Though the hour is extremely urgent and signs of judgment are clearly increasing, there may yet be a small window of hope. While the big picture is profoundly disturbing, some signs point to a growing spirit of prayer and desperation in a small spiritually awakened remnant of believers. And though it may be too late to avoid many difficult events, God often brings great revival out of difficulty! Based on Scripture and current signs, there may yet be hope though times are incredibly urgent. In Scripture, hope for revival always rests on two foundational principles for returning to God.

The Two Essential Steps for Hope and Change!

*(1) We must understand and fully acknowledge precisely "how" we have **departed** from God, **profaned** His name, **offended** His holy nature and **broken** our covenant. We must then corporately and personally repent with great contrition and thoroughness.* Throughout Scripture, we note a dangerous tendency for God's people not to recognize they were under judgment. (Jeremiah 2:23; Malachi 3:7; 1 Corinthians 11:) As believers, it is crucial that we fully "make the connection" it is primarily *our* sin and complacency that has caused America's moral collapse, not the lost people! (2 Chronicles 7:14; Hebrews 10:30-31; 1 Peter 4:17) We must discern exactly how we departed from God and the specific steps necessary to return. Furthermore, we must return by our covenant in Christ's grace, not legalism or self-efforts. But until we understand both the *urgency* and the *exact steps* of repentance, there is little chance of real change. This book is prayerfully designed to produce deep brokenness and clearly outline the precise steps of repentance. I have sought to be specific and

very thorough. Nothing less than full repentance will suffice before God.

In Scripture, God's people in sinful decline often either ignored, minimized or denied their sins. Their typical defensive response was, *"In what way have we departed?"* (Jeremiah 2:23; Malachi 3:7) Until they personally identified and fully repented of their "specific" sins, there was no revival. Above all, genuine repentance must be specific, personal, corporate and *very* thorough. Effective repentance is never casual, general or shallow. It must also be a repentance for the right reasons — the glory and pleasure of God. Since God doesn't change His core principles, the same pattern will surely prove true today. *"I am the Lord God, I change not!"*(Malachi 3:6; James 1:17)

To do anything less than fervent prayer and repentance is to demonstrate a dangerous complacency and over-reliance on our own abilities. It is vital that saints understand the full seriousness of self-reliance and complacency before God. We must turn from the prideful self-reliance of trying to minister with only a passing emphasis on prayer and no focus on deep repentance. Though we may "say" humbling ourselves in prayer and repentance are crucial, it is our actual "practice" that reveals the truth. It is as if many think programs, promotion and training can somehow replace biblical fullness of the Holy Spirit. While much of the neglect is unintentional, it is nonetheless very real.

Until believers realize shallow prayer, complacency and self-reliance deeply offend Christ, we are not likely to seriously repent. (Revelation 3:15) One thing is certain — God will never share His glory with men, programs or books. (1 Corinthians 1:29) He steadfastly resists even the slightest hint of pride or self-reliance. (1 Peter 5:5) While we generally don't "intend" to be self-reliant, a lack of prayerful repentance strongly suggests these elements are present.

In many ways, our greatest need is to grasp the full desperation of modern conditions. Dear saints, once we realize our actual condition, there can be no proper response but profound brokenness, deepest humility and prayerful repentance. To do less is to shamefully sleep while society fast approaches a coming cliff. Leaders if we ignore or gloss over current reality, we are dangerously similar (if not identical) to the false prophets of old. To fail to declare fully God's message is to shamefully betray God and His people.

The Danger of Silence About God's Judgment

Crucial to a modern solution is a huge increase of religious leaders who fully understand and boldly proclaim God's message of repentance to the Church. As leaders, among our biggest responsibilities is to arise and call churches to deep brokenness and repentance over current conditions. It is also our responsibility to help people know exactly "how" to repent. One thing is certain — God's people almost never become burdened and repentant until their leaders become broken and call solemn assemblies! Throughout Scripture, leaders that misguided God's people did so by focusing mostly on positive projections of "blessing and peace" (though God was actually about to bring judgment.)

False leaders in Scripture typically shared mostly what the people wanted to hear and were out of touch with God's true message. (Isaiah 30:10) Though what they were saying was often technically biblical, it was simply not God's primary word to that particular people at that time. In essence, they were sharing what they "hoped" was true rather than what God was actually saying. It is even quite possible many of these prophets actually believed their projections of peace, blessing and staying the course (though some no doubt knew their error.) Every Christian leader needs a profound awareness it is easy to (unwillingly) drift into the same subtle patterns of false prophecy.

Rejecting Today's False Prophecy Syndrome
"Smooth Words and Untempored Mortar"
(Jeremiah 6:14; Ezekiel 13:1-16)

Many false prophets likely do not realize they are false. While trying to "accentuate the positive" (or perhaps bolster their own positions) they inadvertently obscured the true conditions of danger. Modern leaders can easily be affected by the same pressure to "seem successful" and "keep people positive." Many succumb to the powerful (though subtle) pressure to bow to the crowds who want their preachers to bring "smooth words." (Isaiah 30:10) Smooth words mean messages that are mostly "pleasant and affirming," not "convicting, challenging or God-exalting." Today it might be expressed by those who say, "I just want to bring messages of hope and affirmation." That's great unless God is actually seeking to bring a word of urgent warning and repentance. (Which He almost surely is.)

Like the false prophets of old, it is very easy to begin "plastering with untempored mortar" and "healing my peoples' wounds slightly" by somewhat glossing over sin. (Jeremiah 6:14; Ezekiel 13:1-16) If we give people shallow answers that don't go far enough, we are falling into the same deadly pattern. In a desire to be encouraging and hopeful, we may well be trying to affirm and comfort a people God is seeking to break and convict. Regardless of the motive, failing to declare the whole truth is both misleading and damaging. With false prophecy, the problem is often "what is left unsaid" as much as what is "said." The error is stopping short of *full* repentance and adequate adjustments. False prophets more or less "gloss over" sin and suggest shallow "half-measure" solutions. Any calls to repentance are mostly general and non-specific. They further suggest God will surely hear our prayers (though we are seriously compromised, apathetic and unyielded in heart.)

"Healing My Peoples' Wound Slightly"
Declaring Peace and Safety in Front of an Iceberg
(Isaiah 30:10)

While it is certainly important to continually praise God for blessing and celebrate progress, faithful leaders *must* keep their eyes squarely on the "big picture" of actual conditions. Though often unintentional, it is easy to drift into an over-celebration of results and patterns (that are actually very low.) One of the worst things we could do is exaggerate how "well we're doing" while mostly *glossing over* the hard realities and signs of a coming storm. Though it hurts us to do so, for God's sake and the good of the people, we must be diligent and faithful to declare God's "whole council." (Not just pleasant words of our own choosing.)

It is vital that we resist the temptation to "focus only on a few modest positives while our people rapidly drift toward a coming spiritual cliff. Faithful and wise leaders tell the whole truth and present the "big picture" of God's heart and central message. They prepare and guide God's people into thorough repentance. Rather than put their heads in the sand or give up, they look beyond immediate surface events and prepare people to seriously seek God. True messengers see beyond the present to God's word for coming days.

God's messengers also do not promote mere surface prayers and shallow confession while ignoring a rising flood of evil. Conversely, false prophets focus only on the "now" and tell people mostly what they want to hear. Any repentance they do suggest is typically general, surface and incomplete. It is often more about stopping potential discomforts than truly returning to God Himself. In light of the gathering floods of spiritual darkness, how can we do less than sound the call to urgent repentance and prayer? Indeed, we must shout the call to return with *all* our hearts! To do less is to shamefully betray God, this generation and those to come.

Yet astoundingly, many today are actually hesitant to suggest God could soon bring judgment on a sleeping Church and vile nation. In light of today's horrific conditions, how could we possibly think He *wouldn't* send judgment? How can we not declare His whole truth? Yet it seems for many, the desire is for easier crowds and broad popularity more than faithfulness to God. It is deeply disturbing to see some evangelical leaders appear on secular talk shows and back-pedal about God's judgment. It is evident they are ashamed to state clear scriptural truth and feel they need to apologize or sanitize God's reputation. It is deeply troubling when we are ashamed to state what God clearly says about Himself. As preachers and denomination leaders, we must ask ourselves the following question. "To whom am I mostly loyal — God, myself or the people?" God alone is to be our primary loyalty! Anything less is blatant idolatry and false prophecy.

The Greatest Need of the Hour
Clear Prophets and Bold, Faithful Leaders
(Hosea 4:6)

Currently, there is a desperate need for leaders to arise and boldly present the full truth of God's message to this generation. In light of current realities, it is time to sound every alarm bell. To do anything less is to shamefully betray our responsibility to God, the Church and this generation. Leaders, we must not so focus on a few "mercy drops" that churches become overconfident and neglectful of the need for profound brokenness, repentance and prayer. It is utterly essential to now call believers to deep contrition, humble repentance and fervent prayer that brings revival. Leaders if we continue to do less, our hands will surely be stained with the blood of this generation! (Ezekiel 33:8) God forbid that it must be said of our generation, *"My people are destroyed for lack of knowledge."* (Hosea 4:6)

To be biblical, today's call to prayer, repentance and holiness must be *intense, specific* and *sustained.* True revival never comes through temporary token themes we promote and quickly drop. Though this book will almost certainly draw attack from some, I am utterly *compelled* to write it. To do anything less would be lulling people to sleep with a deadly iceberg directly ahead. To ignore current and coming conditions is to become a false prophet. Ultimately, there is only One to whom every leader, preacher and writer will answer. Brethren, our responsibility is to speak *His* words, not ours! (Isaiah 58:1, 13)

Beyond question, this same responsibility is squarely upon all who lead God's people. And in reality, every believer *is* a leader and influencer of someone. To fail to fully instruct and warn God's people is to drift into the patterns of the false prophets. Saints, we must come to realize false prophecy is not only proclaiming doctrinal heresy, it is also simply failing to declare God's whole message or His immediate focus. Today, many have drifted into false prophecy though what they are declaring is basically biblical and on other occasions, might be God's actual message. (But it is not God's central message to the current setting!) Again, it's often what we're leaving unsaid that becomes our condemnation and the destruction of those under our care. This brings us to a second essential step for hope and change.

(2) We must reject today's pervasive spiritual shallowness and return to deeper prayer intimacy with God and each other. Now is the time to embrace an intense call to return to God with "all our hearts." (Jeremiah 29:13) In today's Church, it is vital that we embrace a much deeper level of personal and corporate prayer with full repentance. Generations never "drift"

into Great Awakenings. They come by the "rending of hearts" in profound God-seeking repentance, *not* brief, casual prayer. (Joel 2:12-20)[72] Yet today's more surface studies and shallow calls to commitment have essentially "dumbed down" many modern saints (in a spiritual sense.) In other words, we have far too often taught and expected only the lowest levels of commitment, discipleship and prayer. Even much of what we are calling discipleship is more studying "about" discipleship than actually doing it. Unlike the early Church, many today have seriously "watered down" expectations and standards. As a result, multitudes have become spiritually stunted at very low levels of growth.

Churches must return to the top priority teaching of truly fervent prayer, full surrender to Christ's Lordship and deep passion for souls. We simply cannot continue to marginalize prayer and ignore repentance. Make no mistake — full power in the *great commission* requires the *great submission* to Christ's Lordship. (Matthew 6:33; John 15:4-8; Acts 1:4-8) Though we have a myriad of elaborate strategies and promotions, full New Testament power comes *only* by deep spiritual cleansing and prayer! If there is to be any hope of revival, modern saints must again be challenged (and equipped) to move beyond shallow three minute quiet times that contain little real confession, repentance or kingdom intercession.

Restoring Deep Cleansing, Joy and Empowerment
"The Heart of Joyful Abiding in Christ"

Today's outreach, preaching, teaching and ministry efforts *must* start to include far more than a brief pause for prayer! Without deeper prayer *and* cleansing, ministry efforts will surely lack the full power of the Holy Spirit. The Lord strongly stressed our complete inability to do spiritual work without His fullness and power. (Acts 1:4-8; John 15:4-8; Ephesians 5:18)

Thus it is both astounding and disturbing that virtually no modern outreach or ministry preparations include thorough cleansing as a vital part of participants' preparation. Leaders, do we seriously think our people can know true fullness of the Spirit without deep cleansing and surrender? Are we unaware that we must (above all) seek and secure the biblical fullness of the Holy Spirit?

Our conspicuous neglect reveals a significant misunderstanding of true spiritual power. Indeed, if any generation ever needed to stress deep cleansing and surrender, it is surely ours! Today's neglect essentially *guarantees* leaders and workers are functioning without the biblical fullness and power of God's Spirit (no matter how well we can recite outlines, construct sermons, run programs or work lesson plans.)

Believers, we simply *must* incorporate deeper prayer and thorough cleansing into every part of our lives, ministries and strategies! (Psalms 66:18; John 15:4-8) Indeed, fervent prayer, deep cleansing and full surrender should always be essential preparation for any effort in preaching, teaching and witnessing. Only then can we know the fullness and power of God's Spirit. Saints, we either really need this element or we don't. I frankly can't image anyone trying to argue that we really don't need deeper levels of spiritual cleansing, fullness and power. Yet one thing is certain — deep spiritual cleansing is almost wholly ignored in the preparation and training for our vital ministries!

Churches must further embrace kingdom-focused prayer meetings and periodic corporate repentance. (2 Chronicles 7:14; Matthew 21:13) Righting strained relationships must also become a central priority among today's division-torn saints. (Matthew 5:23; 6:14; John 13:34-35: 17:21) Saints, these elements are not just "important," they are "absolutely essential" for experiencing God in true revival and evangelistic power! These "relational foundations" are unquestionably our missing elements. Until we choose to seriously return to God by these paths, our efforts are much like "painting deck chairs on the *Titanic*." (It's simply not going to make much long-term difference.)

Preparing for "Significant" Change
(Not Just Token Lip Service)

Even as some now claim a readiness to repent and seek God for revival, the question is whether we are prepared to repent *enough* to really see one. The answer depends on how much we are prepared to face today's full extremity of desperation. Unfortunately, with many conventions and promotions, it is easy to so accentuate a few modest positives that we in effect "gloss over" the true bigger picture. Though somewhat unintentional, it is easy to leave the impression the latest book or strategic plan is the "magic bullet" (though dozens of promising promotions have come and gone before it.)

While it is certainly important to create and promote better ministry strategies, marginalizing prayer and omitting repentance actually "desensitize" and "inoculate" churches to the desperate need for God's manifest power. Even when prayer is part of a strategy, deep cleansing of heart is often wholly ignored. How could we think we don't need deep cleansing? Such patterns surely doom us to minimal results. After all, God is unspeakably holy and prayer without deep repentance is very limited in power. Shallow emphases leave the false impression that a little casual prayer and brief (or no) confession is all we really need.

It is further true that some promotions inadvertently give the impression we're doing much better than we really are. After all, actual baptisms and lasting results are always the true measures, not promotional hype. The way some denominations selectively report (or don't report) statistics also desensitizes believers to the real picture. But why are such patterns a concern? Desensitization is a concern because it gives a dangerously false picture of our true condition. Thus, it keeps believers from the serious brokenness, prayer and repentance that is utterly essential to all Great Awakenings! We also may cross into the dangerous realms of self-reliance and exaggeration. Throughout Scripture, God is very resistant and reactive to even small elements of fleshly self-reliance, bragging or exaggeration of our own strengths. (Judges 7:2; 2 Samuel 24:10; James 4:6; 1 Peter 5:5; Revelation 3:15-18)

Brokenness and Humble Dependence
"Crucial Missing Keys to Modern Revival"

Throughout all history, a central element of returning to God is deep brokenness and humble contrition. So how about it? Do you think the American Church is sufficiently broken, humbled and desperate to alter some of our "busyness" and seek God with "all our hearts?" Do we really understand the awesome holiness of God? Are key leaders ready to call serious sustained prayer and biblical solemn assemblies? Are we at last prepared to *"fast and weep between the porch of the altar?"* (Joel 2:18) Is our current level of focus on prayer and repentance sufficiently desperate to bring a Great Awakening? Are we ready to seek the glory of God's Name and spread of His kingdom more than temporal needs and comforts? Sadly, by most indicators the answer to each question is still an emphatic no.[5]

Yet, there are at least some signs of hope! A small but growing remnant *is* seeking God as never before. More and more leaders and layman are realizing, "we've literally tried everything yet actual results reveal an ever-worsening moral collapse." There is at last a dawning awareness new programs or better promotions are *not* the primary answers. Godly pastors and leaders are increasingly hungry for true spiritual intimacy and New Testament empowerment in Jesus.

However, if we are to see explosive evangelism and revival, history suggests the number of burdened laymen and leaders must yet rise significantly.

If today's small seeking remnant is to grow into a mighty sweeping movement, the truth of our spiritually bankrupt condition must fully dawn on greater numbers. The fact God is deeply grieved and offended must utterly grip our hearts. Whether or not we realize it, we *are* utterly desperate for another historic move of God! We are desperate for His mercy and manifest presence. In Matthew 16:1-3, Jesus clearly called His people to "discern the true signs of the times." As pastors and leaders, our primary job is to help God's people do just that! So how about it leaders? What are the current signs and what are they telling us? What time is it spiritually? While there are some positive signs, the preponderance of indicators point to a desperate and unprecedented urgency. Without a passion to return to God in deeper prayer and repentance, we will almost surely experience far worse moral collapse and judgment.

Today's Most Pressing Needs
Heart Passion and Evangelistic Power!
(Not Just More Programs)

Based on recent history and current spiritual declines, it is incumbent that believers return to joyful, empowered intimacy with God. We must quickly come to realize it is primarily fervent prayer and full surrender to Christ that create heart passion and power, *not* mere strategies and promotions! *In other words, we cannot "program, promote or train" our way into true heart passion, repentance and power.* One thing is certain — today's powerlessness and apathy are *not* from a lack of tools, education, training or promotion. Indeed, our most obvious need is an explosion of true heart motivation and passion for God. Only deep abiding closeness with Jesus brings that!

Our generation must quickly awaken to the reality that programs do not (by themselves) create spiritual power and heart passion for souls — intimacy with Jesus does! If there is to be hope for revival, we cannot continue to spend ninety-five percent of our focus on promotional strategies and five percent on half-hearted prayer and shallow (or no) repentance. We must return to the top priority teaching and practice of deep prayer, thorough repentance and joyful intimacy with Jesus! Only true closeness with Jesus can bring passion and power to human hearts.

In light of fifty years of seriously declining baptism and growth ratios, it quite clear simply *pushing harder* or *pedaling faster* is obviously not the central answer. Neither is tossing in a little casual prayer while essentially ignoring deep cleansing and repentance. I am aware some sincere souls may object to these statements by suggesting that "we *have* included emphases on prayer and repentance." Yet today's error is one of faulty definitions and lack of power. In other words, what *we* typically mean by powerful prayer and repentance and what *God* means in Scripture are very different. It is essential that we avoid the subtle arrogance (and inaccuracy) of asserting that we have adequately focused on prayer and repentance. Merely having a few events or adopting a temporary theme cannot suffice. We must embrace a strong commitment to change "foundational patterns" of practice. To do less is to fall victim to a subtle (but deadly) spiritual inoculation syndrome.

Recognizing Today's Spiritual "Inoculation Syndrome"
A Subtle But Deadly Pattern

Unfortunately, the modern understanding of prayer and repentance is generally quite shallow when compared to the generations, leaders and nations that actually experienced history's Great Awakenings. Many in our generation are seriously affected by a spiritual "inoculation syndrome." In physical inoculation, people receive a weakened version of an organism that prevents them from getting the real thing. Let me explain. In the spiritual realm, this occurs when we embrace today's somewhat weakened, generalized versions of prayer and repentance. Consequently, when prayer and repentance mostly skim the surface, we simply don't experience full cleansing or complete surrender to God. In effect, today's shallower practices of prayer and repentance are actually keeping us *from* experiencing the full power of God. (It is deceptive because we "think" we have adequately prayed and repented.)

In most modern approaches and patterns, we are unquestionably stopping short of the deeper prayer and repentance historically required for full New Testament power. Unfortunately, all the programs in the world cannot substitute for truly powerful prayer and deeply cleansed hearts. *Only* these bring full New Testament power and sweeping revival! (2 Chronicles 7:14; Jeremiah 29:13; Joel 2:12-19; James 4:8-10) Beyond question, today's serious lack of depth and power has brought us to the very brink of spiritual disaster.

This same deadly scenario can also happen in evangelistic efforts and preaching. For example, sharing gospel presentations that are excessively shallow can easily get people to make "decisions" that fail to convert the soul. They are then ensnared in the dangerous position of thinking they are saved when in fact, they are not. In a real and deadly sense, they are now "inoculated." Modern statistics leave no doubt millions have made "decisions" and joined churches without true new birth conversion. On this and many other levels, the American Church has reached a point of unparallel urgency.

Sound the Alarm
Spiritual Iceberg Dead Ahead!

Under the next heading, I thoroughly describe several of today's most poignant signs of the times. I almost sense I need to warn readers before they read the coming section. If some want to keep their heads in the sand and continue thinking "we're doing alright," they should stop reading right now. What you are about to read reflects nothing less than a catastrophic moral and spiritual collapse. Even more disturbing is the fact these elements are only now beginning to converge in a deadly cycle of *escalating cumulative impact.* This means multiple factors are reaching a point when negative changes do not merely increase, they start compounding *exponentially!*

It is especially sobering to realize with most of today's disturbing signs, the larger impact is just "beginning" to move into patterns of full development. As younger generations start voting and seniors rapidly die off, we will begin to see the impact of having law-makers who were raised in extreme spiritual darkness. It is somewhat like "falling off a cliff" morally and spiritually. We may fast be approaching the pattern of the "sudden destruction" described in Proverbs 29:1 *"He who is often rebuked, and hardens his neck, Will suddenly be destroyed, and that without remedy."* In the analogy of the Titanic, it is colliding with an iceberg in the middle of the Atlantic Ocean. Based on the appalling moral state of current conditions, we are indeed living on "borrowed time" concerning sins cumulative consequences and God's judgment. Current sign's foretell a *far* greater explosion of darkness if we do not soon see a huge Great Awakening.

How Could God *Not* Be Judging Us?

Of even greater concern is the fact several of today's conditions are classic signs of increasing biblical judgment.

With today's appalling conditions, it is frankly surprising any believer would ask, "*Could* God be judging us?" In light of a sleeping, compromised Church and vile nation, the more appropriate question is, "How could He *not* be judging us?" While most believers realize things are bad, most have no idea just *how* bad they really are.

As readers consider the coming signs, our true condition will become painfully evident. While there are some positive signs (which I will outline later), today's few modest positives do not even begin to match the rising tidal wave of decline. Though God could reverse all these evil trends with a wave of His mighty hand, He generally acts only as His people seriously seek His face. Fervent prayer and deep repentance are God's *only* paths to revival closeness with Himself. Saints, let us immediately "discern the times" and humble our hearts before God.

A Time to Rend Our Hearts
Yet From Brokenness Springs Hope!
(Joel 2:12-18)

I firmly believe the next few months and years may well be our "last chance" to avert total spiritual disaster. In fact, before this book is far distributed, severe new trials may have already broken upon our land. In light of exploding signs of spiritual devastation, we simply do not have another five or ten years to continue programs and promotions as usual! Dear saints, we are far past being much helped by mercy drops — we must see a mighty flood of God! We cannot afford to settle for an occasional, fleeting two or three percent baptism increase. It is essential that we experience the *two to four hundred percent increases* of a Great Awakening. In some revivals, the baptisms and growth percentages were even far higher! Only a truly major awakening has any chance of reversing today's exploding flood of evil. And such awakenings come only by

God's appointed means — profound repentance, fervent prayer, Spirit-led contrition and biblical fasting. But thank God, great awakenings can come in the very blackest of conditions. By His grace we *can* pray and repent on deeper levels. There is no better way to end this book than the very words of our great God.

God's Word to Generations in Decline

"If My people who are called by My name will humble themselves, and pray and seek My face, and turn from their wicked ways, then I will hear from heaven, and will forgive their sin and heal their land." (2 Chronicles 7:14)

"Now, therefore," says the LORD, "Turn to Me with all your heart, With fasting, with weeping, and with mourning." So rend your heart, and not your garments; Return to the LORD your God, For He is gracious and merciful, Slow to anger, and of great kindness; And He relents from doing harm. Who knows if He will turn and relent, And leave a blessing behind Him—A grain offering and a drink offering For the LORD your God? Blow the trumpet in Zion, Consecrate a fast, Call a sacred assembly; Gather the people, Sanctify the congregation, Assemble the elders, Gather the children and nursing babes; Let the bridegroom go out from his chamber, And the bride from her dressing room. Let the priests, who minister to the LORD, Weep between the porch and the altar; Let them say, "Spare Your people, O LORD, And do not give Your heritage to reproach, That the nations should rule over them. Why should they say among the peoples, 'Where is their God?'" Then the LORD will be zealous for His land, And pity His people." (Joel 2:12-18)

"Sow for yourselves righteousness; Reap in mercy; Break up your fallow ground, For it is time to seek the LORD, Till He comes and rains righteousness on you." (Hosea 10:12)

"Therefore say to them, 'Thus says the LORD of hosts: "Return to Me," says the LORD of hosts, "and I will return to you," says the LORD of hosts." (Zechariah 1:3)

"I know thy words, that thou art neither cold nor hot; I would thou wert cold or hot. So then because thou art lukewarm, and nether cold not hot, I will spue thee out of my mouth. Because thou sayest, I am rich, and increased with goods, and have need of nothing: and knowest not that thou art wretched, and miserable, and poor, and blind, and naked. I counsel thee to buy of 0me gold tried in the fire, that thou mayest be rich; and white raiment, that thou mayest be clothed, and that the shame of thy nakedness do not appear: and anoint thine eyes with eye-salve, that thou mayest see." (Revelation 3:15-18)

Appendices

Appendix A

Evidence of a Coming Iceberg
Thirty-One Signs of Spiritual Desperation and Rising Judgment

This appendix is a summarized listing of thirty-one key indicators of moral, spiritual and social conditions. The signs not only indicate our present position but also the rapid changes that are steadily escalating. In the analogy of this book, the signs outline the devastating spiritual iceberg directly in our path. Any thoughtful reader will be struck by the severity and totality of current conditions.

The signs you are about to read are disturbing. In fact, what you read may well be history's worst spiritual collapse in such a short period of time. The speed and totality of the signs illustrates an unusual exponential escalation of evil conditions. Yet the purpose of this appendix is not to discourage but rather to awaken and motivate God's saints. It is a call to humble ourselves and seek God with all our hearts! May God grant us true brokenness and determination to see revival in our day.

Signs in the Moral and Social Realm
"Shocking Occurrences on Our Spiritual Watch"

1. Over the last fifty years, biblical morality, marriage patterns and family strength have not merely declined, they have witnessed an unprecedented collapse. Worse yet, this unprecedented collapse has now permeated very deep into modern churches.
2. Reverential fear of God, respect for Christ's Church, belief in the Bible and regard for Christians has plummeted to shockingly low levels. Vast percentages no longer have any real sense of sins' accountability to the holy God Who judges all wickedness. They fear neither sin's consequences nor God's righteousness judgment.

3. In just one generation evil has not simply increased, it has become "many times" more brazen, blasphemous, perverted and accepted! Both the phenomenal speed and totality of today's collapse is most unusual in Christian history. What we are seeking is not a typical spiritual downturn. It is a full-blown "values reversal" where good is viewed as evil and evil as good!

4. Television, movies and the Internet have exploded pornography and perversion far beyond anything we could have even imagined just ten years ago. In all history, there has likely not been anything like today's pervasive media utterly saturating society with moral and spiritual filth. No propaganda machine in history has ever equaled modern media.

5. In a remarkably short time period, America has witnessed a massive, unprecedented cultural shift away from a Judeo-Christian world-view and biblical values. It is rare to have ever seen societal attitudes and beliefs decline so much so fast. To move from the America of the 1950's to today's America is virtually unwitnessed in history.

6. As the more biblically oriented senior adult voters now rapidly die-off, America is on the verge of a huge negative shift in the morality, world-view and personal values of voters who elect government and set policies. Without a massive spiritual awakening, tomorrow's government and laws will bear little resemblance to the America we have known.

7. Large percentages of the Mosaic and Baby Buster generations are profoundly impacted by education, music and entertainment industries that are overwhelmingly anti-moral and anti-Christ. Consequently, their attitudes, beliefs and values are markedly different than the older age groups (that are now so rapidly dying off.) The profoundly negative impact on attitudes and beliefs is severe and growing with alarming speed.

Signs in Churches and Religion
As Go The Churches — So Goes Society!

8. A large majority of churches and denominations are about to be hit by a serious demographic "age bomb." American churches have never experienced such a dramatic loss of a single age

group that comprises so much congregational leadership and financial support. Without a massive spiritual awakening, the soon coming demographic shift will severely impact church attendance, financial support, missions and congregational leadership.

9. In spite of a population that had doubled in fifty years, nation-wide baptism and church growth ratios have experienced unprecedented stagnation and decline. At present, an astounding 70-80 percent of American churches are either plateaued or declining. Of the smaller percentage that are actually growing, significant numbers are by no means growing at rates equal to population expansion. Furthermore, we are losing significantly more churches than we are starting. In spite of all our churches, North America is the only continent in which the Church is not growing!

10. An honest analysis and full breakdown of most church (and denominational) baptisms reveals a shocking lack of impact in evangelizing the truly unchurched. Aside from membership transfers and biological baptisms, lasting adult outreach conversions are phenomenally low.

11. It is incredibly significant and alarming that America's baptism ratio decline and moral collapse has seriously escalated "despite" a much increased, twenty-five year emphasis on prayer, revival and spiritual awakening. While major prayer movements of the past produced huge explosions of genuine baptisms and vibrant church growth, most modern indicators have badly declined.

12. Several major Christian denominations have experienced devastating division over issues as foundational as simple morality and even the most basic belief in the authority of Scripture. Throughout all history, no group that seriously doubted Scripture has ever witnessed sweeping revival. In fact, doubting Scripture virtually always brings devastating spiritual decline and weakness.

13. Extremely high levels of church and denominational bickering, division and splits reveal shocking degrees of carnality in many modern saints. Not only is bickering rampant, many churches have functioned more as inward-focused social clubs than red hot seekers after the souls of men. Virtually nothing more shames

God's name or hinders evangelism than today's widespread church disunity and self-focused temporal priorities.

14. In disturbing numbers of churches, foundational ministries such as mid-week prayer meetings, evening worship, Sunday School, serious discipleship, expository Bible preaching and revivals majoring on repentance have either seriously declined or wholly disappeared.

15. The last twenty years represent by far the biggest explosion of moral failures and public scandals among high profile Christian leaders and pastors.

16. In most denominations, alarmingly high numbers of pastors and leaders are nearing retirement age. Catholics and many Protestant groups are facing a fast-rising crisis of biblically qualified clergy and lay leadership.

17. In terms of growth percentages, several cults, new age groups, atheists and false religions have seen unprecedented expansion while many evangelical denominations have witnessed unprecedented stagnation and decline.

18. Of the relatively small minority of churches that are actually growing, troubling numbers are doing so at the expense of healthy balance, biblical holiness and depth of discipleship. Some have adopted new approaches and philosophies with dangerous levels of Scriptural imbalance.

19. The overwhelming majority of today's "growing churches" require locations where population growth is rapidly exploding around them. Today's patterns are almost a tragic opposite of those of the early Church and churches of Great Awakenings. They grew by thousands of lasting adult conversions in the very worst of locations with extreme cultural, government and religious opposition.

20. Today's generation has produced an unprecedented explosion of new theories and innovative methods for growing churches. Unfortunately, several are biblically unbalanced and violate basic spiritual principles for New Testament, revived churches.

Signs in Church and Leadership Priorities
Discerning "Why" We Have Come to the Current Collapse

21. Modern churches have been seriously weakened by a "skewed reference point" concerning evangelism, revival and church norms. In essence, modern saints almost entirely lost a truly biblical and historic "reference point" for spiritual success and supernatural power. We have begun to measure ourselves by ourselves rather than Scripture and revival history. Such patterns greatly damage a revival-producing spirit of faith and expectancy.

22. During the last sixty years, many churches (and denominations) embraced ministry models and patterns seriously inadequate for New Testament power, full Spirit-guidance and true revival. When we lost God's foundational biblical patterns for churches, we lost His full manifest presence. In essence, most settled for ministry models that marginalized (or neglected) intense prayer, deep repentance and biblical unity. These patterns are no doubt largely responsible for our current condition.

23. Over the last six decades, busy believers (and many leaders) gravitated toward excessively brief personal devotions instead of substantial time in Scripture, prayer, fasting and cleansing. As a result, we lost the experience of true biblical power and fullness in Christ.

24. A troubling number of pastors and leaders have embraced personal ministry models that major much more on human leadership principles and organizational techniques than intense prayer, spiritual empowerment and deep holiness before God. When leadership models are more humanistic and organizational than God-focused and spiritual, true revival power is impossible.

25. Over the last century, an overwhelming majority of churches almost completely abandoned powerful, church-wide prayer meetings. Throughout Scripture and history, churches without powerful corporate prayer are churches without God's revival presence! Dynamic corporate prayer is a *non-negotiable* essential for truly revived, New Testament churches!

26. Over the past century, the vast majority of churches abandoned periodic revivals that focused on deep, Bible-based cleansing and thorough church-wide repentance among saints. Churches

without deep holiness and fear (reverence) of God are churches without full New Testament power. Periodic, Spirit-guided cleansing is a *non-negotiable* essential for truly revived, New Testament churches!

27. There is very strong indication the American Church contains an alarming number of unconverted members. Evidence further suggests many who are indeed saved, do not have "full assurance" of salvation and thus lack overcoming power and victory.

28. Over the past century, much preaching moved away from proclaiming sound Scriptural theology, biblical grace, a high view of God, hallowing His name, sin's accountability and strong expository preaching of God's "whole council." In essence, many have unwittingly sought to create a "god" in their own image. The subtle attitude is to have God serve us rather than us serve Him.

29. Many American churches became so micro-managed and rigid in their worship and prayer scheduling, they essentially "programmed" God right out of the mix. While revival "requires" serious opportunities for deep encounter, the vast majority of churches have no open-ended services or prayer meetings where people are encouraged (and led) to truly respond to God.

30. Many churches became more programmed and formula-focused than genuinely God-centered and Spirit-guided in receiving His unique vision for them. Rather than truly seeking and hearing God themselves, they merely plug in the latest program, fad or book study. Unfortunately, there are no "short-cuts" to true revival or deep intimacy with Christ.

31. Classic signs of biblical judgment have rapidly increased and loom very heavy on the near horizon. America and the western Church now have virtually all of the key biblical indicators of likely judgment from God. By many indicators, we have already come through several stages of judgment and are on the edge of far worse. *For clarity, I list the basic signs under the next heading.*

Ten Signs of Worsening Judgments
"The Biblical Warnings Signs"

(1) America and many churches have unquestionably moved far into the two conditions that bring an extremely heightened risk for destructive consequences and judgment. (The conditions are blatant rebellion in spite of great blessing and full knowledge of God's will.) (Proverbs 29:1; Jeremiah 2:4-13; Luke 12:47-48; Hebrews 10:26)

(2) Statistics show a significant majority of churches are spiritually weak and virtually powerless to turn today's rushing tide of evil. (Joshua 7:1-13)

(3) The last twenty years represent by far our severest collapse of morals and family life. We have also witnessed a catastrophic decline in the numbers that hold a biblical world view. Vast numbers have lost any fear and reverence for God, His word or His work. (Psalms 11:3; Romans 1:20-30; Proverbs 14:34)

(4) Today, we are witnessing an astoundingly rapid proliferation of highly motivated, empowered political, social and religious enemies. (Isaiah 5:1-7; Jeremiah 6:19-23)

(5) We now see the election of increasingly immoral, anti-Christian leaders who will do or say anything to get elected. (Isaiah 5:20; Romans 1:28)

(6) Currently, there is serious confusion and seeming irrationality among many religious, government and financial leaders. (Job 12:20-25; Micah 3:1-8)

(7) Today we are witnessing an unprecedented explosion of political and religious scandals. Evil self-serving leaders are frequent signs of God's judging of a nation. (Jeremiah 5:30-31)

(8) At present, our nation is plunging toward massive infrastructure crises of our own making. Irresponsible leaders are frequent signs of God's withheld blessing and protection.

(9) Through lack of moral will, politics and sheer foolishness, modern leaders have ignored national border integrity until it has become a desperate, fast worsening crisis.

(10) We have witnessed a disturbing rise in unusually devastating natural and human-caused disasters (with exponentially greater potential on the immediate horizon.)

Appendix B

Covenants of Prayer for the Lost and Spiritual Awakening

My Acts 1:8 Prayer Covenant
"The effective, fervent prayer of the righteous is powerful."
(James 5:16b)

Dear Father, because you have commanded us to witness to all the world and make disciples, *I covenant to do five things*. (1) I will daily embrace Your cleansing, fullness and power. (2) I will pray for myself and my church to have a missional focus and aggressively witness to all the world. (3) I will fervently pray for my list of lost souls and ever seek ways to bring them to Christ. (4) I will seek to be a daily witness wherever I go. (5) I will give sacrificially to evangelism and missions.

How to Effectively Pray for the Lost

† Pray for their hearts to be *deeply convicted of sin* and lostness (John 16:8)

† Pray for God to *open their eyes* and *reveal Christ* as Lord and Savior (Matthew 16:17; 2 Corinthians 4:4)

† Pray for them to be overwhelmingly *drawn to Christ* by God's Spirit (John 6:44)

† Pray for God to *tear down any barriers* keeping them from salvation (1 Corinthians 10:5)

† Pray for God to make their hearts *good soil* fully receptive to Christ (Matthew 13:8)

† Pray for God to grant them the *new birth* and *true repentance* (2 Corinthians 5:17; Luke 13:3)

† Pray that they *become fruitful disciples* that lead others to Christ (Matthew 28:18-20; John 15:8)

Souls I Covenant to Daily Lift to God

_____

_____

_____

_____

My Prayer Covenant for Revival and Spiritual Awakening

With morals collapsing and judgment rising, it is essential that God's millions unite in the effective, fervent prayer of clean hears. (2 Chronicles 7:14; Matthew 18:19; James 5:16) There is enormous power when believers covenant together in fervent, united prayer and repentance! Yet it is also vital that we pray with biblical depth and effectiveness. The following prayers are both biblical and complete in reflecting God's heart. Prayerfully adopt the following covenant. **I covenant with God and millions of saints to pray these prayers until God *"rends the heavens."*** (Isaiah 64:1)

Seven Covenant Prayers for Revival and Spiritual Awakening

1. Pray for God to have *mercy* and move believers to true *brokenness and humility* (2 Chronicles 7:14; Jeremiah 29:13)
2. Pray for *love, repentance* and *holy fear* to grip God's people (Matthew 22:37-39; 2 Corinthians 7:1)
3. Pray for a strong *faith* and *intercession* to fill God's people (Matthew 21:13; Acts 2:1; Hebrews 11:6)
4. Pray for *holiness, boldness* and *power* in God's leaders and churches (Acts 1:8; 1 Corinthians 2:4)
5. Pray for *loving unity* and *oneness* to engulf Christ's Church (John 13:34; Acts 2:42-47)
6. Pray for burning *passion* and *power* in evangelism and missions (Matthew 28:18-20; Acts 1:8)
7. Pray for God to *"rend the heavens"* in *sweeping revival* and *spiritual awakening* (2 Chronicles 7:14; Isaiah 64:1; Psalms 85:6)

"If My people who are called by My name will humble themselves, and pray and seek My face, and turn from their wicked ways, then I will hear from heaven, and will forgive their sin and heal their land." (2 Chronicles 7:14)

"Will You not revive us again, That Your people may rejoice in You? Show us Your mercy, LORD, And grant us Your salvation." (Psalms 85:6-7)

"Oh, that You would rend the heavens! That You would come down! That the mountains might shake at Your presence." (Isaiah 64:1)

Appendix C

Restoring Revived New Testament Churches
Recapturing the Seven Essential Priorities

It is my strong conviction churches should embrace seven basic priorities. In light of Jesus' statement in Matthew 21:13, we surely cannot view prayer as a periphery issue unworthy of primary focus. *"My house shall be called a house of prayer."* Neither can we function as if churches do not need periodic times of special cleansing and renewal. In Scripture, prayer and periodic repentance are definitely important enough to warrant continual top priority emphasis. Yet in most churches, these vital emphases receive little real priority focus. In the following paragraphs, we examine simple ways to restore the key missing elements of revived New Testament churches.

I realize for some it might seem unnecessary to treat prayer and periodic spiritual cleansing as distinct points of priority focus. Yet based on Scripture and revival history, there has virtually never been Great Spiritual Awakening unless these practices were front and center! Believers, if we are to have any chance of seeing explosive growth, mass evangelism and renewal, we simply *must* recapture these elements as top priorities.

Beyond question, it is not enough to simply assume casual, indirect focus is sufficient. If you doubt this assertion, we have fifty years of moral and spiritual collapse to prove our need to return to the seven priorities. If focusing on the five priorities alone could bring revival, it would have long since done so! And yet there is great news concerning these issues. Recapturing greater prayer and cleansing are *not* complicated or out of reach. And at last, some are doing just that!

The seven areas of priority can serve as an excellent evaluation guide for assessing your general church health. With each of the seven areas, simply rate your current strength and evaluate any need for growth. In the evaluation question, rate your need from 1 to 10. (1 meaning we need little or no focus and 10 meaning an extensive, urgent need.) These seven priorities should be a guide for greater effectiveness and growth, not a source of condemnation or despair. Remember, we serve a gracious God and wonderful Shepherd. With the right priority and focus, God will surely lead our churches to growth and strength!

Why We *Must* Take the Seven Priorities Seriously
"The Essence of God's Manifest Presence"

Before we examine the seven church priorities, I urge readers to take the additional two priorities (prayer and repentance) very seriously. After all, the past fifty years of decline definitively prove the five basic purposes (without deep prayer and repentance) are *not* enough. In actuality, deeper prayer and repentance provide the power for the other basic priorities! Prayer and repentance are the very heart of corporate intimacy with God.

Friends, if we continue to do the five purposes, without fervent prayer and surrender, we are doomed to continue with far less than New Testament impact. Indeed, the first two elements are the essential "relational triggers" to the empowerment of our efforts! They are the essence of God's presence released in our midst. And here is some great news — *any* church and pastor can incorporate prayer and repentance as a stronger priority! But one thing is certain — if we are to have any hope of significant change, we must make these adjustments.

The Clear Proof of Scripture and History
Patterns and Truths We Cannot Ignore!

If any believer doubts the importance of churches returning to a priority focus on prayer and repentance, Scripture and history should remove all reservations. The point becomes clear by answering these simple questions. (1) What was the precise way God brought all twelve major revivals of the Old Testament? (2) What were the primary patterns that caused the awesome power in the early Church? (3) What was God's specific principle in all of history's Great Spiritual Awakenings? The answer for all three questions is exactly the same. *They united God's people in fervent prayer, deep spiritual cleansing and clear preaching of God's word!*

Dear readers, because there has never been great empowerment and renewal without intense prayer and repentance, why in the world would we think we can neglect them as central priorities? Why would we think we can just throw them into the mix? Apparently, we forgot the most essential elements of full power and closeness with God. Though some would argue we haven't forgotten the elements, we have certainly marginalized them. And yet there is hope. By returning to the following pattern, we will recapture full closeness and power with God! (Joel 2:12-18; James 4:8-10)

Put simply, if a church places consistent serious emphasis on the seven essential priorities, it will be blessed and empowered by God. It will bear *"much fruit that remains."* (John 15:16) While churches do not have to be perfect in all seven, they do have to be intentional and serious. Consider the following priorities as something of a church compass and biblical plumb line.

The Seven Essentials of Church Priority Focus

1. **Personal and Corporate Prayer** – *Powerful, New Testament churches place a major sustained focus on corporate and personal prayer.* (Mark 11:17; Acts 2:1, 42-47; 4:31-32; James 5:16)
2. **Personal and Corporate Repentance** – *Powerful New Testament churches understand the importance of periodic, God-directed times for deep spiritual cleansing and renewal.* (2 Chronicles 7:14; Joel 2:12-18; 2 Corinthians 7:1)
3. **Fellowship/Loving Unity** – *Powerful New Testament churches have strong patterns of loving fellowship and caring ministry.* (John 13:34-35; 17:21; Acts 2:42-47; 1 Corinthians 12-14)
4. **Evangelism and Missions** – *Powerful New Testament churches place enormous focus on evangelism and missions.* (Matthew 28:18-20; Acts 1:8)
5. **Discipleship — Bible-Centered Preaching and Teaching** – *Powerful New Testament churches embrace the dynamic preaching of God's "whole counsel."* (Acts 20:27; 2 Timothy 3:16)
6. **Ministry/God-Revealed Vision** – *Powerful New Testament churches have a strong God-given, kingdom-focused vision for their ministry.* (Proverbs 29:18; Matthew 6:33; Ephesians 5:17)
7. **Worship in Spirit and Truth** – *Powerful New Testament churches place a strong priority on ever-deepening patterns of worship.* (Psalms 100:4-5; John 4:23; Hebrews 13:15)

The Seven Essentials of Church Priority Explained

1. **Personal and Corporate Prayer** – *Powerful, New Testament churches place a major sustained focus on*

corporate and personal prayer. (Mark 11:17; Acts 2:1, 42-47; 4:31-32; James 5:16) According to Scripture, united prayer is absolutely crucial to full church empowerment and fellowship. Like perhaps nothing else, corporate prayer is God's primary means of manifesting His awesome presence among His people. Personal and corporate prayer are the very heart of our power and closeness with Jesus. For these reasons, it is essential to seek a pastor who continually develops *strong* personal and corporate prayer in his people. The pastor must treat this as an "actual" ongoing priority rather than one he merely "states."

Developing dynamic personal and corporate prayer is by far the biggest failure of most modern pastors and churches. Today's conspicuous lack of fervent prayer meetings is no doubt a huge reason for low baptisms and spiritual weakness among churches. Corporate prayer and repentance are among the primary ways we humble ourselves and hallow God's holy name. These are essential expressions of reverential awe (fear) of God which we must regain!

Effective churches and pastors find ways to consistently address the need for stronger prayer patterns. This emphasis will be a preeminent priority practice, not a periphery side-item. Until churches place top priority focus on corporate and personal prayer, they cannot truly be called New Testament churches. (After all, the New Testament Church was absolutely *saturated* with these elements.)

Concerning powerful prayer meetings, I have great news for every reader. *Any* church can begin to experience dynamic corporate prayer meetings! It is not hard, intimidating or out of reach. Yet because every church is unique, there is no "one size fits all" pattern. For practical help, check out the resource, **Dynamic**

Church Prayer Meetings: *"Why Every Church Should Want Them."* Above all, do not be discouraged. God will surely help you experience His presence as never before. Prayerfully answer the following questions for evaluation.

Questions For Church Evaluation and Growth: Is our church seeing strong measure growth in personal and corporate prayer? _____ Do we view dynamic personal and corporate prayer as top priorities or do these areas need greater focus? _____

2.   **Personal and Corporate Repentance** – *Powerful New Testament churches understand the importance of periodic, God-directed times for deep spiritual cleansing and renewal.* (2 Chronicles 7:14; Joel 2:12-18; 2 Corinthians 7:1) Periodic, cleansing revivals are a vital biblical pattern for healthy, revived churches. Yet please especially note the phase "God-directed" cleansing and renewal. I am referring to the pattern of letting God lead us to these times, not doing it by set calendar or program. But make no mistake — the element of deep cleansing is indeed a non-negotiable principle for full revival closeness with God! In light of today's moral and social climate, it is absolutely essential for modern congregations to recapture this largely abandoned principle. Of course, by revival and repentance, I do not mean the typical evangelistic campaign. I refer to a church-wide process to take believers through deep spiritual examination and cleansing in all areas of their lives (i.e. attitudes, thoughts, words, relationships, actions, omissions, full surrender, etc.)

Though to some this process may sound impractical, negative or intimidating, it really isn't.

There are some fairly simple and practical ways churches can be led into deep times of renewal. Churches should seek a pastor who can lead the church into genuine periodic cleansing and revival. Effective pastors know how to emphasize a type of revival that is based on grace and joy, not legalism. Indeed, real revival is based on love and grace, not condemnation. For practical help check out the resource, **Cleanse Me O God:** *"Journey to Genuine Revival and Wholeness."* Prayerfully answer the following questions for evaluation.

Questions For Church Evaluation and Growth: Is our church seeing strong growth in its patterns of deep spiritual cleansing and true revival? _____ Do we view spiritual cleansing and revival as major priorities or is this an area needing greater focus? _____

3. **Fellowship/Loving Unity** – *Powerful New Testament churches have strong patterns of loving fellowship and caring ministry.* (John 13:34-35; 17:21; Acts 2:42-47; 1 Corinthians 12-14) In several passages, Jesus actually tied our evangelistic witness and spiritual power to deep love and unity among believers. Indeed, if church relationships are strained, God's Spirit is seriously quenched. Thus if God's Spirit is quenched, evangelism is hindered and Christ's name is dishonored. Beyond question, loving unity is essential to our power! It is also crucial to the glory we bring to God's name. Little profanes God's name more than bickering and fighting among saints. While certainly no church is perfect, the right leaders can help churches maintain a loving fellowship.

For this reason, it is vital to find a pastor committed to developing strategies for relational oneness, loving fellowship, united vision and consistent ministry to the hurting. Healthy churches have an atmosphere of loving fellowship, caring ministry and God-given, kingdom vision. But make no mistake, healthy unity and fellowship do not happen by accident. A prospective pastor must be committed to guide the church in ministering to all the needs of the flock (i.e. spiritual, emotional, relation, financial, physical, etc.) While he certainly does not try to do it all himself, he takes strong measures to mobilize the whole body to ministry. He will also be committed to minister to all age groups. Prayerfully answer the following questions for evaluation and growth.

Questions For Church Evaluation and Growth: Is our church strong and growing in loving fellowship and mutual ministry? _____ Do we need to place greater priority and leadership toward our fellowship, unity and care ministry? _____

4.   **Evangelism and Missions** – *Powerful New Testament churches place enormous focus on evangelism and missions.* (Matthew 28:18-20; Acts 1:8) Seek a pastor committed to preaching evangelistically, developing strong outreach strategies, Sunday school, soul winning, evangelistic campaigns and strong baptism patterns. He should be strongly committed to developing powerful local, state and foreign missions projects. It is my conviction the Acts 1:8 pattern is a primary biblical model for missional focus (i.e. Jerusalem, Judea, Samaria, uttermost parts of the earth — local community, association, state, national, world) While this is not to be treated as a rigid program, it is a healthy priority and biblical direction. We must also understand we cannot do Acts 1:8 until we experience

Acts 1:4 and 4:31-32 (deep prayer, surrender and spiritual fullness.)

Until churches place intense priority focus on evangelism and missions, they really cannot be called New Testament churches. After all, the early Church was utterly centered around evangelism and missions. While inward focused churches tend toward spiritual dryness and bickering, kingdom-focused churches are alive and unified around touching lives. It is vital to find a pastor with an intense kingdom focus. Prayerfully answer the following questions for evaluation and growth.

Questions For Church Evaluation and Growth: Is our church seeing strong growth and blessing upon our evangelism, discipleship and missions activities? _____ How does our baptism pattern compare with the average for a church our size? _____ Are these areas in which we need greater priority focus and leadership? _____

5. **Discipleship — Bible-Centered Preaching and Teaching** – *Powerful New Testament churches embrace the dynamic preaching of God's "whole counsel."* (Acts 20:27; 2 Timothy 3:16) It is essential to seek a pastor committed to expository preaching of balanced doctrine and biblical theology. Truly biblical pastors will preach and teach to a wide range of needs, doctrines and theology (rather than a few popular topics.) Is he committed to developing strong Sunday school, discipleship training, personal growth, marriage emphases, stewardship training, special needs focus, etc.? These are crucial questions for any prospective pastor or church.

Especially in a day of shallow, self-focused preaching, it is vital to see churches return to genuine discipleship. In many respects, many modern saints actually need to be reintroduced to the God of Scripture. Much preaching has so majored on God's love, believers are ignorant of His various other attributes. In essence, many have sought to create a God in "their own image" rather than proclaim the God of Scripture. There is little question that revival will require a return to the reverential fear (awe and respect) of God. We must have preachers that preach the entire Bible and the whole nature of God. To do less, is to move toward the realm of false prophecy. Prayerfully answer the following questions for evaluation and growth.

Questions For Church Evaluation and Growth: Are we committed to pulpit ministry that preaches the whole counsel of God in balanced discipleship, evangelism, theology and biblical exposition? _____ Do we need to seek a higher standard in preaching and teaching the whole Bible? _____

6. **Ministry/God-Revealed Vision** – *Powerful New Testament churches have a strong God-given, kingdom-focused vision for their ministry.* (Proverbs 29:18; Matthew 6:33; Ephesians 5:17) It is vital to find a pastor committed to seek God's strategic ministry vision for the congregation. Such a pastor will lead the church in a comprehensive God-given vision that is both local and global. (The Acts 1:8 pattern.) We simply must find a pastor who knows the difference between embracing human strategies and receiving a God-revealed vision. (Though part of God's vision may well be books and strategies.) Truly effective churches

(and pastors) know how to receive God's unique direction and plan for their own congregation. A God-given vision is more than just embracing the latest book. Since every church has uniqueness, it is vital to seek God's unique direction. Prayerfully answer the following questions for evaluation and growth.

Questions For Church Evaluation and Growth: Does our church have a strong kingdom vision and concrete strategic goals? _____ Do we view Spirit-led strategic vision as a top priority or is this an area needing growth? _____

7.   **Worship in Spirit and Truth** – *Powerful New Testament churches place a strong priority on ever-deepening patterns of worship.* (Psalms 100:4-5; John 4:23; Hebrews 13:15) There is no question that true worship is central to our very purpose. It is also true that genuine worship is crucial to the release of God's full manifest presence. (Psalms 22:3) For this reason, churches must seek a pastor committed to leading the church to ever stronger patterns of worship and music ministries. Yet, he must know how to change and grow in music without alienating large portions of the congregation.

We must determine if a prospective pastor views worship as more about music styles or about biblical content and God-focus. The goal is to find a pastor who realizes worship in Spirit and Truth is far more than certain music styles. I further stress that worship does not need huge numbers or spectacular orchestration to be incredibly dynamic! When worship is genuine, Spirit-led, solid in content, it will be powerful. While music and style is important, true worship is ultimately a matter of heart and obedience. (Matthew 15:8)

Prayerfully answer the following questions for evaluation and growth.

Questions For Church Evaluation and Growth: Are we seeing significant growth in the balance, depth and quality of our worship? _____ Are we moving to greater unity concerning our worship? _____ Is deeper worship a need for greater priority focus and leadership? _____

Appendix D

Steps for Repentance and Change
Resources for Practical Help

In this Appendix, I identify specific steps of repentance for six of the key patterns described in Chapter Three. Along with each pattern, I list powerful resources that provide practical help for targeting the issues. While the soon coming (expanded) **Iceberg Dead Ahead** will go into much greater detail, these sample steps are enough to begin major changes.

There is no question God will mightily bless obedience in the areas we have long neglected. May God give us the determination to return to His essential paths. Prayerfully consider the following steps and resources.

Sign Twenty Two
Restoring the Relational Foundations and Seven Essentials

In order to return to God in true repentance, we must first understand how we departed. As mentioned throughout this book, our primary departure was an abandonment of the "relational foundations" and "seven essential priorities" of New Testament churches. One thing is certain — the early Church and all churches of revival strongly emphasized three things alongside evangelism. They emphasized: (a) personal and corporate prayer, (b) personal and corporate repentance and (c) relational unity of believers. They also practiced all seven essentials of revived churches. These *are* the crucial elements of truly abiding in Christ! The following are essential steps of biblical repentance with suggested resources to help.

(1) **Individuals** *must embrace a lifestyle that includes a strong personal prayer life, effective spiritual cleansing and reconciliation of any damaged relationships.* While such a life of abiding is not hard or time prohibitive, it does take more than today's average three minute devotion. Going deeper with God requires a commitment to specific steps of adjustment. The following resources will help believers move into far deeper prayer. *Resource for Implementation* — **How to Develop a Powerful Prayer Life** and **Returning to Holiness** by Gregory Frizzell; **The Life-Changing Power of Prayer** by T W. Hunt, **Experiencing Prayer with Jesus** by Henry and Norman Blackaby.

(2) **Pastors** *and* **churches** *must embrace a church ministry model (or strategy) that includes the relational foundations and essential priorities with the basic five purposes.* While we certainly still focus on the five purposes, we bring much stronger focus on prayer, deep periodic repentance and relational unity. *Resources for Implementation* — **Iceberg**

Dead Ahead (expanded version, 2008); **Appendix C** of this book; **Dynamic Church Prayer Meetings and Solemn Assemblies** all by Gregory Frizzell; **The God-Focused Church** by Henry and Melvin Blackaby.

Sign Twenty Three
Embracing Powerful Prayer and Abiding In Christ

In today's fast-paced, instant society, it is vital that believers return to truly effective prayer and intimacy with Christ. Only then can we have the abiding fullness of the Holy Spirit as described in Acts 1:8 and John 15:4-8. Yet there is good news. Every believer and leader can learn to experience powerful prayer and cleansing, joyful intimacy with the Savior.

The following resources will help revolutionize any Christian's walk with God. *Resources for Implementation* — **How to Develop a Powerful Prayer Life**, **Abiding in Christ** and **Powerful Kingdom Prayers for Every Believer** by Gregory Frizzell; **The Disciple's Prayer Life** and **The Life-Changing Power of Prayer** by T. W. Hunt; **Mighty Prevailing Prayer** by Wesley Duewel.

Sign Twenty Four
Restoring Biblical Leadership Models

Before any leaders can discern whether his or her leadership strategies are adequate, they must understand the essential biblical patterns for empowered leaders. With today's explosion of different approaches and philosophies, it is vital that we have the foundational principles firmly in our minds and heart. Otherwise, we will be tossed from one good sounding idea to the next.

Under sign Twenty Four (in Chapter Three), I fully described the essential elements of a biblical leadership model. Yet even in busy modern society, we can still embrace New Testament models for truly empowered leaders. Prayerfully consider the following steps for returning to the New Testament leadership pattern.

(1) Let deep intimacy, power with Christ and daily fullness of the Holy Spirit become your central leadership strategy.

(2) Reject today's brief devotional prayer models and embrace significant time in fervent prayer, deep cleansing and biblical fasting.

(3) Study the lives and patterns of great revivalists and anointed spiritual leaders throughout Church history. Take careful note of how they prayed, their personal holiness, their preaching and how they led people.

(4) Reject any excuse suggesting "things are different now" or that your main gifts are strategies, not personal closeness and deep fullness in Christ.

Resources for Implementation — **Spiritual Leadership:** *Moving People in to God's Agenda* by Henry and Richard Blackaby; **The Man God Uses:** *Moved from the Ordinary to the Extraordinary* by Henry Blackaby; **Holiness and Power in Christian Leaders** by Gregory Frizzell. (This tool guides leaders in a journey of deep cleansing, powerful prayer and a strong re-focus on ministering through Christ's empowerment.) **Empower Us O God!** *"Acts 1:8 Power in a Modern Day World"* by Gregory Frizzell.

Sign Twenty Five
Restoring Powerful Church Prayer Meetings

Perhaps the single most destructive of all church changes has been the abandonment of dynamic corporate prayer. Both Scripture and history leave no doubt that powerful united prayer is to be a continual top priority for all churches. It is certainly a central priority in virtually all churches of Great Spiritual Awakenings. Yet for a variety of reasons, most modern churches almost totally abandoned this all-important element of intimacy and power with God.

But again, there is very good news. God is restoring this priority in growing numbers of pastors! And beyond question, any church can take powerful steps in corporate prayer. Though each pastor will follow God's unique method and timing, all churches can take steps of obedience in corporate prayer. The results are worth it a hundred times over! Prayerfully consider the following steps of obedience.

(1) Take a month or two and teach the congregation about the power and biblical importance of church prayer meetings. The preaching (or teaching) series should be combined with all members reading **Dynamic Church Prayer Meetings: *"Why Every Church Should Want Them!"*** (released summer 2008) This tool is designed to motivate church members to desire church prayer meetings and help them understand their importance. The book is also designed to eliminate any of their fears and prevent opposition or boycotts.

(2) Commit to let God guide you into the best patterns for moving your church into dynamic corporate prayer meetings. (The recommended resources can help with that problem.) Since every church is

different, pastors will let God lead to the right approach and timing.

(3) Begin a powerful prayer group (or groups) as well as a regular church-wide prayer meeting. Some churches may be led to start with prayer groups and later move to a church-wide prayer meeting.

(4) Make sure the prayer meetings are Spirit-guided and kingdom-focused. Use the prayer meeting as a primary way to grow your people in effective prayer and cleansing before God.

Resources for Implementation — **Dynamic Church Prayer Meetings** by Gregory Frizzell - This major book is unique in that it is designed for whole churches to study and become excited about starting the prayer meeting. It not only educates, it greatly inspires and helps prevent opposition. **Evangelistic, Kingdom-Focused Church Prayer Meetings** also by Gregory Frizzell - This practical tool provides a variety of ways churches can develop corporate praying, worship service prayers and evangelistic prayer groups. **Prayzing from A to Z** by Daniel Henderson - This tool contains a wealth of great ideas for combining prayer with worship. **And the Place Was Shaken** by John Franklin - This tool is a solid biblical description of the importance and practicality of corporate and small group prayer. **Prayer Prompts for Church Prayer Meetings** by Chris Schofield – This small booklet is packed with dynamic ways to enlist kingdom-focused prayer with other believers. (For information contact the North Carolina Baptist Convention.)

Sign Twenty Six
Restoring Church-wide Cleansing, Unity and Renewal

As well as neglected prayer meetings, most American congregations abandoned church cleansing revivals and solemn assemblies. It is also crucial to conduct times of relational healing and restored unity. These events are non-negotiable elements of truly revived New Testament churches. Prayerfully consider the following steps for repentance and revival.

(1)   Conduct periodic church-wide emphases of deep spiritual examination and repentance. (Of course, this is done at God's leading in the ways He directs.)

(2)   Take Lord's Supper much more seriously as a time for deep examination and repentance.

(3)   In addition to general church-wide cleansing and repentance, conduct special emphases totally focused on healing broken relationships and deepening unity.

Resources for Implementation – **Returning to Holiness: "*A Personal and Church-wide Journey to Revival*"** by Gregory Frizzell. This tool contains five practical patterns for conducting solemn assemblies, biblical revivals and various cleansing/renewal emphases. **Miraculous Church Unity: "*Journey to Healed Relationships and Revival*"** by Gregory Frizzell; **Fresh Encounter** by Henry Blackaby and Claude King; **The Solemn Assembly** by Richard Owen Roberts.

Sign Twenty Seven
"Restoring Biblical Salvation and Full Assurance"

A huge problem in the American Church is the prevalence of lost church members and doubting saints. Adding to the problem is that many lost church members don't realize they are lost and many doubting saints don't know why they doubt. It is further true that most believers do not have strong prayer lives or walk in victory.

If there is to be revival, the issues of salvation, assurance and victory are central! To powerfully address these foundational issues, it is crucial that churches make adjustments. Key steps and resources are crucial to the process. Prayerfully consider the following steps and resources.

1. Conduct a major multi-week series of sermons or studies on salvation, certainty and spiritual victory. Any such emphases should be bathed in prayer.

2. Conduct an evangelistic crusade (or event) using a balanced, biblical evangelist, not a manipulator.

Resources for Implementation — **Saved, Certain and Transformed:** *"Journey to Biblical Salvation, Full Assurance and Personal Revival"* by Gregory Frizzell. This balanced tool is powerful for converting lost church members, delivering doubting saints and bringing all saints into dynamic prayer and victory. It contains a powerful church-wide prayer strategy. **How to Know You Are a Christian** by Donald Whitney. This is an excellent tool for study or teaching.

Notes

Introduction

1. Lord, Walter. *The Night Lives On "New Thoughts, Theories, and Revelations About the Titanic* (New York, William Morrow & Company, Inc., 1986) 69
2. Kunty, Tom. *The Titanic Disaster Hearings: The Official Transcript of the 1912 Senate Investigation"* Hearing before a Subcommittee of the Committee on Commerce, US Senate 62nd Congress, second session, S RES 283 (New York, Pocket Books, a division of Simon & Schuster, Inc. 1991) 61
3. Titanic Chronology: A Clear Timeline of Events Related to the RMS Titanic http/www.titanic-nautical.com/RMS-Titanic-Chronologoy.html.
4. Whiting, Jim. The Sinking of the Titanic (Hockessin, Mitchell Lane Publishers, 2007) 9-10
5. See note 1 above, 59
6. Edward, Brian. *Revival: A People Saturated with God* (Durham, Evangelical Press, 1990), 38-39
7. Blackaby, Henry and Claude King. *Fresh Encounter* (Nashville, Broadman & Holman Publishers,1996) 88
8. Willis, Avery, e-mail message to author, September 20, 2007
9. Roberts, Richard Owen *Repentance: "The First Word of the Gospel"* (Wheaton, Good News Publishers, 2002) 16
10. See note 3 above
11. Frizzell, Gregory. *Returning to Holiness: "A Personal and Church-wide Journey to Revival"* (Memphis, The Master Design, 2000) 11
12.
13. Frizzell, Gregory. *Seeking the Reviver, Not Just Revival* (Oklahoma City, Baptist General Convention of Oklahoma, 2005)

14. Roach, Erin. Culture Digest: Barna: American Christianity a lukewarm church. (Baptist Press, May 30, 2007) http://www.bpnews.net

15. Graf, Jonathan. "God Is Up to Something!" *Pray Magazine*, March/April 1999 http://www.navpress.com/EPubs; Fuller, Cheri, "Tidal Waves" *Pray Magazine*, September/October, 2002 http://navpress.com/EPubs

16. Your "Pastors' Prayer Group" Connection, National Pastors' Prayer Network, http://www.nppn.org/PPG.htm

17. Internet

18. HBI Global Partners, e-mail message to author, July 27, 2007

19. Fuller, Cheri. Tidal Waves "Teens Making a Difference on Their Campuses," *Pray Magazine,* September/October, 2002 Issue 32, http://www.navpress.com/EPubs

20. Campbell, Duncan. *The Nature of God-Sent Revival* (Montvale, VA: Christ Life Publications n.d.), 10

Chapter One

21. Number of Divorces and Annulments Divorce and Annulment Rate Michigan and United States Occurrences, Selected Years 1900-2005, http://www.mdch.state.mi.us/PHA/OSR/marriage/Tab3.5.aasp.

22. Smart Marriages Archive, reproduced in the Divorce Statistics Collection, (Associated Press, December 30, 1999) http://www.divorceform.org/mel/rbaptisthigh.html

23. Popenoe, David. The State of Our Unions The Social Health of Marriage in America 2007 Essay: The Future of Marriage in America, http://marriage.rutgers.edu/Publications.SOOU/Textsoou2007.htm

24. Popenoe, David. Marriage Decline in America: Testimony Before Subcommittee of Human Resources, Committee on Ways and Means, US House of Representatives, May 20, 2001.

25. US Census Bureau, US Department of Commerce 2000, American's Families and Living Arrangements; Stanley, Richie, Comparison of Changes in population, Southern Baptist Churches and Resident Members by Region and State, 1990 to 2000, http://www.namb.net/site/apps/nl/content2>asp?.

26. National Vital Statistics Reports, Volume 48, No 16, October 18, 2000

27. Project Safe Haven, Internet Pornography Statistics and Other Statistics – The Scope of the Problem, http://www.1wayout.org/pages/PrintStatistics.aspx; National Center for Missing & Exploited Children, Child Pornography Possessors Arrested in Internet Related Crimes: Findings from the National Juvenile Online Victimization Study, Virginia National Center for Missing & Exploited Children, 2005); Roach, David, US Awash in Porn, (Baptist Press, August 21, 2007) http://www.bpnews.net/printerfriendly.asp?ID=26286

28. Kunkel, Dale. PhD, Keren Eyal, Ph.D., Keli Finnerty, Erica Biely and Edward Donnerstein, PhD, Sex on Tv4, (The Henry J. Kaiser Family Foundation, 2005) 57-60

29. Hart, Dr. Archibald D., The Hart Report: Confidential Survey of 600 Ministers, printed by the Sexual Man, (Word Publishing, 1994) 119.

30. Wheeler, Mark. PG-13 Films Not Save for Kids, University of California, Los Angeles School of Public Health, June 7, 2007 http://www.ph.ucla.edu/pr/newsitem060706.html

31. Flynn, Sean, "Is Gambling Good for America?" *Parade Magazine*, May 20, 2007, 4

32. FBI Report: Crime in the United States, 2006, Expanded Homicide Data Table 3, and Expanded Homicide Date Table 3 for 2005

33. Transforming Culture: Christian Truth Confronts Post-Christian America, http://www.albertmohler.com/article

34. Barrick, Audrey, Study: Fewer Americans Embrace Traditional View of God, (Christian Post, May 22, 2007), http://www.christianpost.com/pages/print.htm?aid=27546

35. Barrick, Audrey, "Study: Fewer American Embrace Traditional View of God." (Christian Post, Mary 22, 2007) http://www.christianpost.com/pages/print.htm?Aid=27546

36. Ibid.

37. LifeWay news office, "Research Reveals Why Young Adults Drop Out Of Church," Baptist and Reflector, August 15, 2007

38. Roach, Erin. Culture Digest: Most professors hold unfavorable view of evangelicals, study says. (Baptist Press, May 16, 2007) http://www.bpnews.net

39. Carlson, Doug. Debate on Criminalizing Religious Thoughts, Speech Draws Near. (The Ethics & Religious Liberty Commission, August 21, 2007) http://www.erlc.com/article/debate-on-criminalizing-religious-thoughts-speech-draws-near

40.

Chapter Two

41. Jones, Phillip. *Southern Baptist Congregations Today Research Report*, (North American Mission Board, February, 2001) 37; Church Attendance Research Archive (Barna Research), http://www.barna.org/FlexPage.aspx?Page=BarnaUdateNarrow&BarnaUpdateID=216&P_

42. Stewardship Research Archive (Barna Research), http://www.brana.org?FlexPage.aspx?Page=BarnaUpdate Narrow&BarnaUpdateID=216&P
43. Ibid.
44. Smith, James A., Sr., "Scholar Offer Reasons for SBC Stagnant Baptism Statistics and 'Modest Proposal' for Improvement," Florida Baptist Web Exclusive Witness, April 28, 2005, http://www.floridabaptistwisness.com/4249.article
45. Grossman, Cathy Lnn. "Rites of Baptism Trickles Away," USA Today, April 12, 2006 http://www.usatoday.com/news/religion/2006-04-12-baptism-trend_x.html
46. US Bureau of Census, Current Population Report, P25-917 and P25-1095, and Population Paper Listing No. 21.
47.
48. Stetzer, Ed, Disturbing Trends in Baptists, October 25, 2006, http://www.namb.net/site/apps/nl/content2.asp
49.
50.
51.
52.
53. Barnes, Rebecca and Lindy Lowry, Special Report: The American Church in Crisis, May/June 2006 (Christianity Today.com) http://www.christianitytoday.com/global/printer.html?outreach/articles
54. Bloom, Linda, UMNS Report: United Methodist Church Membership Drops Below 8 Million, June 21, 2006 http://www.namb.net/site/apps; Change, Pauline J., Presbyterian Membership Drop Hits Record Low, The Christian Post, June 3, 2006 http://www.namb.net/site/apps; World Christian Database: Denominations by Size (Protestants by Country) February 8, 2004, http://ww.worldchristiananddatabase.org/wcd/esweb.asp
55.

56. see note 21 above
57. Benson, Ron, "The Alban Institute estimates that many pastors are experiencing burnout," *Christianity Today*, October 18, 2003 http://www.namb.net/ site/apps/n1/contents2.asp
58. Dart, John, "Stressed Out: Why pastors leave," Pulpit&Pew, November 29, 2003, http://www.pulpitandpew.duke.edu/Stressed.htm
59. Barnes, Rebecca, "Clergy shortage remains despite increase in Christian college enrollment," http://www.namb.net/site/apps
60.
61.
62.
63.
64.
65.

Chapter Three

66. Deming, Melissa, "Special Report: Unregenerate church member might spell R.I.P. for SBC," (TEXAN, December 11, 2006) http://www.ministrycraft.com/ clienttools/ printarticle.asp?; Pierce, Jerry, Special Report: Born-Again Baptists? (TEXAN, December 11, 2006) http://www.ministrycraft.com/ clienttools/printarticle.asp?
67.

Chapter Four

68.
69.
70. Knox, Noelie, "Religion takes a back seat in Western Europe," USA Today, August 10, 2005,

http://www.usatoday.com/news/world/2005-08-10-europe-religion-cover_x.htm.

71.

72.

Study Notes